Concurrent Programming

26 Cambridge Computer Science Texts

Concurrent Programming

C. R. Snow

University of Newcastle upon Tyne

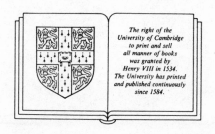

The right of the
University of Cambridge
to print and sell
all manner of books
was granted by
Henry VIII in 1534.
The University has printed
and published continuously
since 1584.

Cambridge University Press

Cambridge

New York   Port Chester   Melbourne   Sydney

Published by the Press Syndicate of the University of Cambridge
The Pitt Building, Trumpington Street, Cambridge CB2 1RP
40 West 20th Street, New York, NY 10011-4211, USA
10 Stamford Road, Oakleigh, Victoria 3166, Australia

© Cambridge University Press 1992

First published 1992

Printed in Great Britain at the University Press, Cambridge

Library of Congress cataloguing in publication data available

British Library cataloguing in publication data available

ISBN 0 521 32796 2 hardback
ISBN 0 521 33993 6 paperback

Contents

Preface

For a number of years, Concurrent Programming was considered only to arise as a component in the study of Operating Systems. To some extent this attitude is understandable, in that matters concerning the scheduling of concurrent activity on a limited number (often one!) of processing units, and the detection/prevention of deadlock, are still regarded as the responsibility of an operating system. Historically, it is also the case that concurrent activity within a computing system was provided exclusively by the operating system for its own purposes, such as supporting multiple concurrent users.

It has become clear in recent years, however, that concurrent programming is a subject of study in its own right, primarily because it is now recognised that the use of parallelism can be beneficial as much to the applications programmer as it is to the systems programmer. It is also now clear that the principles governing the design, and the techniques employed in the implementation of concurrent programs belong more to the study of programming than to the management of the resources of a computer system.

This book is based on a course of lectures given over a number of years initially to third, and more recently to second year undergraduates in Computing Science. True to the origins of the subject, the course began as the first part of a course in operating systems, but was later separated off and has now become part of a course in advanced programming techniques.

We make the assumption that the reader is very familiar with a high-level sequential programming language such as Pascal, and that the examples given throughout the book can be read by a reasonably competent programmer. Certainly, the students to whom the course is given have received a thorough grounding in Pascal programming prior to taking the course.

Sadly, it is still the case that there is very little uniformity about the facilities available (if any) to students wishing to run concurrent programs. It has therefore been rather difficult to provide good programming exercises to accompany the text. Ideally, an environment will be available in which a number of styles of concurrent programming can be tried and compared, but even now such circumstances are rarely available to the average undergraduate class. Encouraging signs are to be seen, however, and concurrency facilities are likely to be available in the most of the next generation of general purpose programming languages which will be candidates for use as first programming languages for student teaching.

Where a system is available which offers facilities for concurrent programming, particularly one which supports the shared memory model, a programming exercise has been suggested (in chapter 3) which may be used to demonstrate the phenomenon of interference (also discussed in chapter 3). A common difficulty in locating bugs in concurrent programs is their reluctance to manifest themselves. It is hoped that this exercise will help to demonstrate that the problem of interference does exist, and that the proposed solutions really do reduce or eliminate the problem.

On the subject of practical work in general, many of the exercises have been constructed in such a way as to suggest that a concurrent program should be written. It is strongly recommended that, if the necessary facilities are available, the exercise solutions should be coded and run, in order to reinforce the points made, and the techniques described in the text.

I have resisted the temptation to include a comprehensive bibliography and have given instead a fairly brief set of references, suitably annotated, which are intended to complement the specific topics covered in the book. A number of these references themselves contain bibliographies of the wider literature on the subject, to which the interested reader is invited to refer.

It is with great pleasure that I acknowledge my gratitude to all those friends and colleagues who have encouraged me through the lengthy gestation period of this book. It is surprising how the simple question "How's the book coming along?" can be a spur to the author. I am also happy to record my thanks to my faithful Xerox 6085 workstation "Brinkburn" running the Viewpoint software, upon which the whole book has been typeset. Finally, this preface would not be complete without recording my enormous appreciation of and thanks to the numberless students who have acted as the sounding board for the views expressed herein. Their reactions to the course, their questions, and to some extent their answers to my questions, have influenced this book in more ways than they, or indeed I, could have realised.

C.R.Snow
Newcastle upon Tyne, June 1991.

1
Introduction to Concurrency

Concurrency has been with us for a long time. The idea of different tasks being carried out at the same time, in order to achieve a particular end result more quickly, has been with us from time immemorial. Sometimes the tasks may be regarded as independent of one another. Two gardeners, one planting potatoes and the other cutting the lawn (provided the potatoes are not to be planted on the lawn!) will complete the two tasks in the time it takes to do just one of them. Sometimes the tasks are dependent upon each other, as in a team activity such as is found in a well-run hospital operating theatre. Here, each member of the team has to co-operate fully with the other members, but each member has his/her own well-defined task to carry out.

Concurrency has also been present in computers for almost as long as computers themselves have existed. Early on in the development of the electronic digital computer it was realised that there was an enormous discrepancy in the speeds of operation of electro-mechanical peripheral devices and the purely electronic central processing unit. The logical resolution of this discrepancy was to allow the peripheral device to operate independently of the central processor, making it feasible for the processor to make productive use of the time that the peripheral device is operating, rather than have to wait until a slow operation has been completed. Over the years, of course, this separation of tasks between different pieces of hardware has been refined to the point where peripherals are sometimes controlled by a dedicated processor which can have the same degree of "intelligence" as the central processor itself.

Even in the case of the two gardeners, where the task that each gardener was given could be considered to be independent of the other, there must be some way in which the two tasks may be initiated. We may imagine that both of the gardeners were originally given their respective tasks by the head gardener who, in consultation with the owner of the garden, determines which tasks need to be done, and who allocates tasks to his under-gardeners. Presumably also, each gardener will report back to the head gardener when he has finished his task, or maybe the head gardener has to enquire continually of his underlings whether they have finished their assigned tasks.

Suppose, however, that our two gardeners were asked to carry out tasks, both of which required the use of the same implement. We could imagine that the lawn-mowing gardener requires a rake to clear some debris from the lawn prior to mowing it, while the potato planter also requires a rake to prepare the potato bed before planting. If the household possessed only a single rake, then one or other gardener might have to wait until the other had finished using it before being able to complete his own task.

This analogy serves to illustrate the ways in which peripheral devices may interact with central processors in computers. Clearly if we are asking for a simple operation to take place, such as a line printer skipping to the top of the next page, or a magnetic tape rewinding, it suffices for the Central Processing Unit (c.p.u.) to initiate the operation and then get on with its own work until the time when either the peripheral device informs the c.p.u. that it has finished (i.e. by an interrupt), or the c.p.u. discovers by (possibly repeated) inspection that the operation is complete (i.e. by polling). Alternatively, the peripheral device may have been asked to read a value from an external medium and place it in a particular memory location. At the same time the processor, which is proceeding in its own time with its own task, may also wish to access the same memory location. Under these circumstances, we would hope that one of the operations would be delayed until the memory location was no longer being used by the other.

1.1   Reasons for Concurrency

Concurrent programming as a discipline has been stimulated primarily by two developments. The first is the concurrency which had been introduced in the hardware, and concurrent programming could be seen as an attempt to generalise the notion of tasks being allowed to proceed largely independently of each other, in order to mimic the relationship between the various hardware components. In particular, the control of a specific hardware component is often a complex task requiring considerable ingenuity on the part of the programmer to produce a software driver for that component. If a way could be found by which those aspects of the driver which are concerned with the concurrent activity of the device might be separated off from other parts in the system, the task is eased tremendously. If concurrent programming is employed, then the programmer can concern himself with the sequential aspects of the device driver, and only later must he face the problem of the interactions of the driver with other components within the system. In addition, any such interactions will be handled in a uniform and (hopefully) well-understood way, so that (device-) specific concurrency problems are avoided.

The second development which leads directly to a consideration of the use of concurrent programming is a rationalisation and extension of the desire to provide an operating system which would allow more than one user to make use of a particular computer at a time. Early time-sharing systems which permitted the simultaneous use of a computer by a number of users often had no means whereby those users (or their programs) could communicate with one another. Any communication which was possible was done at the operating system kernel level, and this was usually a single monolithic program which halted all the user tasks while it was active. Users of such systems were not generally concerned with communicating with each other, and the only form of resource sharing that they required was in the form of competition for resources owned by the operating system. Later systems which came along began to require the possibility of users sharing information amongst themselves, where such information was not necessarily under the control of the operating system. Data could frequently be passed from one user program to another much more conveniently than using a cumbersome mechanism of asking one program to write data into a file to be read by the other program.

The introduction of concurrent programming techniques was also recognised to be a useful tool in providing additional structure to a program. We remarked earlier that the task of constructing a device driver is considerably simplified if the concurrency aspects can be set aside, and then added in a controlled way. This is very similar in concept to some of the well-established techniques of structured programming, in which the communication between the various parts of a (sequential) program is strictly controlled, for example through the use of procedures and parameter lists. Structured programming also leaves open the possiblity of delaying the coding of various parts of the program until a later, more convenient time, allowing the writer of the program to concentrate on the specific task on hand.

In a similar way, the writer of a concurrent program may write a sequential program, leaving aside the questions of the interaction with other concurrently active components until the sequential program is complete and, possibly, partially tested. We suspect that unstructured parallelism in programming would be even more difficult to manage than an unstructured sequential program unless we were able to break down the concurrency into manageable sub-units. Concurrent programming may therefore be regarded as another manifestation of the "divide and conquer" rule of program construction. Such methodologies are also useful as a way of making programs more readable and therefore more maintainable.

1.2   Examples of Concurrency

There are many useful examples of concurrency in everyday life, in addition to the example of the two gardeners mentioned above. Any large project, such as the building of a house, will require some work to go on in parallel with other work. In principle, a project like building a house does not require any concurrent activity, but it is a desirable feature of such a project in that the whole task can be completed in a shorter time by allowing various sub-tasks to be carried out concurrently. There is no reason why the painter cannot paint the outside of the house (weather permitting!), while the plasterer is busy in the upstairs rooms, and the joiner is fitting the kitchen units downstairs. There are however some constraints on the concurrency which is possible. The bricklayer would normally have to wait until the foundations of the house had been laid before he could begin the task of building the walls. The various tasks involved in such a project can usually be regarded as independent of one another, but the scheduling of the tasks is constrained by notions of "task A must be completed before task B can begin".

A second example is that of a railway network. A number of trains may be making journeys within the network, and by contrast with the previous example, when they start and when they end is generally independent of most of the other journeys. Where the journeys do interact though, is at places where routes cross, or use common sections of track for parts of the journeys. We can in this example regard the movement of the trains as programs in execution, and sections of track as the resources which these programs may or may not have to share with other programs.

In some cases, the concurrency is inherent in the situation being considered. Any complex machine, or large plant such as a power station, chemical works or oil refinery, consists of identifiable components which have to be continuously interacting with other components. In a quality-controlled environment, for example, the product of the manufacturing component of the system is subjected to certain test procedures, which in turn provide information which may modify the way in which the manufacturing component behaves. Clearly these two components need to be constantly active and in constant communication with each other for the whole system to work properly.

An example of concurrency directly related to computing and programming can be seen by considering the evaluation of an arithmetic expression. Suppose we wish to evaluate the expression:

$$(a*b + c*d**2)*(g + f*h)$$

We assume that the identifiers a, b, c, etc. have values associated with them, and that the priority rules for evaluation of the expression are as would be expected, i.e. exponentiation first, multiplication second and addition last, modified in the usual way by the inclusion of parentheses. A tree may be drawn (figure 1.1) showing the interdependencies of the sub-expressions within the whole expression, and we may use this tree to identify possible concurrency within the evaluation. Three concurrent evaluations of sub-expressions can begin at once, namely, $a*b$, $d**2$ and $f*h$. When the second and third of these are finished, the multiplication by c, and the addition of g (respectively) can take place, also in parallel. It is only after $c*d**2$

Figure 1.1

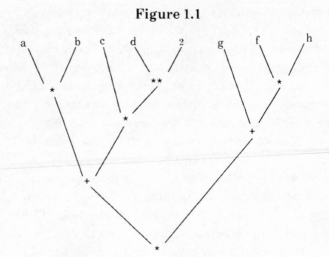

has been evaluated that the sub-expression $a*b$ can be added, and then finally the evaluation of the whole expression can be completed.

It is in the field of operating systems where concurrent programming has been most fruitfully employed. A time-sharing operating system, by its very nature, is required to manage several different tasks in parallel, but even if the system is only providing services to a single user it will be responsible for managing all the peripheral devices as well as servicing the user(s). If the concurrent programming facilities can also be offered to the user, then the flexibility of concurrency as a program structuring technique is also available to application programs. It is not our intention in this book to deal with operating systems as a subject, but it will inevitably be the case that operating systems will provide a fertile source of examples of concurrent programs.

1.3   Concurrency in Programs

Any sequential program is in all probability not necessarily totally sequential. That is, it is often the case that the statements of the program could be re-ordered to some extent without affecting the behaviour of the program. It is usually possible, however, to identify those parts of the program (it is useful to think in terms of program statements in your favourite high-level programming language) which do depend on one another, in the sense that one statement must precede another. A simple example would be the case where a program might include the statement

$$x := x + 1;$$

This statement should really only be used if there has been a previous statement initialising the variable x, e.g.

$$x := 0;$$

We could examine any sequential program and identify all such dependencies, and we would almost certainly find that there were quite a number of pairs of statements for which no such dependencies exist. In other words, it is possible to identify a partial ordering of program statements which define the interdependencies within a program.

Suppose, for example, that a program consisted of statements denoted by the letters $A, B, C, D, E, F, G, H, I$ and J. Suppose also that we were able to write down the partial ordering as a set of relations:

$$A < B, A < C, A < D, C < E, D < E, B < F,$$
$$D < F, E < F, F < G, F < H, G < I, H < J$$

where the relational operator $<$ is meant to be interpreted as "must precede in time". The first property of this partial ordering we notice is that the relation $D < F$ is in fact unnecessary, since it is a consequence of the two relations $D < E$ and $E < F$, this ordering relation having the transitivity property. The partial ordering defined by these relations may be illustrated by a directed graph as shown in figure 1.2.

1.4 An Informal Definition of a Process

It is assumed that any programmer who attempts to write concurrent programs will have had a reasonable amount of experience of conventional sequential programming. With this in mind, we attempt to decompose our concurrent programming problem into a set of sequential programs together with some controlled interaction between them. Thus we put forward as the basic building block of a concurrent program the *sequential process* (where no confusion can

Figure 1.2

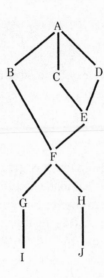

result, we shall abbreviate this to *process*). Perhaps the simplest, and also the least useful definition of a sequential process, is to describe it as the activity performed by a processor. This however begs the question of what is meant by a processor. We have an intuitive notion of what a processor is, namely a device which is capable of performing a sequence of well-defined instructions one at a time. It is largely the case that a sequential process corresponds to an ordinary sequential program, but the use of the word *process* is intended to convey an impression of "activeness" which the word *program* may not. A more formal definition of *process* will be attempted in the following chapter, but for now it will suffice to describe a process as an activation of a program or sub-program. This implies that storage has been made available both for the code being executed and for the data upon which that code operates. It is also useful to think for the moment of the allocated storage space as being distinct from the storage space available to any other process.

Using this notion of the sequential process, we can see that it would be quite possible for two processes to be active at the same time and to be running the same code, i.e. one program can be associated with two distinct processes simultaneously. Conversely, if two programs were to be run strictly sequentially but making use of the same storage area, we might regard them as belonging to the same sequential process. Thus processes and programs are not the same, although clearly "process" would be a somewhat empty concept without an associated program. In the case where two processes are executing identical code, and that code is *pure*, i.e. is never modified as a result of its own execution, then some machines or systems may permit two (or more) processes to access and execute the code from the same physical storage. This has the virtue of saving on actual storage used, but conceptually one should think of separate processes as being totally disjoint and occupying distinct areas of storage.

The question then arises as to how processes are created and how, if at all, they cease to exist. The simplest approach to this problem is to imagine that processes are brought into existence as the system begins to operate, and to continue to exist until the whole system is halted. Such a model has great virtue in the consideration of an operating system, which typically is required to provide services continuously from the starting up of the system to the halting of the machine. Similarly, a general concurrent program may have a fixed number of processes which are initiated as soon as the program starts to run, and remain in existence until the whole program terminates.

Some programming systems, usually in collaboration with the underlying operating system, are capable of creating and destroying processes dynamically. In such cases, the concurrent program clearly has much more flexibility with regard to the way in which processes may be created and destroyed according to the needs of the whole program, and may affect the overall structure of the program.

1.5   Real Concurrency and Pseudo-Concurrency

It is almost always the case that a system allowing the use of multiple concurrent processes (or its users) will require more processes than the number of physical processors provided by the hardware. In those rare cases where the number of concurrent processes is less than the number of available physical processors, we shall refer to the concurrency as *real* or *true* concurrency.

In the more usual situation where the program (or system) requires more processes than there are processors available, in order not to restrict the system arbitrarily, it is necessary that some mechanism be provided which will simulate the action of a number of processes using a single processor only. This may be achieved by running the processor under the control of a (preferably small) program commonly known as a *kernel*. The responsibilities of the kernel will vary from system to system, but it must provide the abstraction of multiple concurrent processes. This is usually implemented using some kind of *time division multiplexing* of the processor. Concurrency provided in this way will be referred to as *pseudo-concurrency*. A kernel which provides only the multiple-processor abstraction is actually not very useful, and so in general a kernel will also offer some form of inter-process communication mechanism, and possibly some primitive operations to allow the dynamic creation and deletion of processes. We shall discuss the implementation of a kernel in a later chapter, and it is sufficient to note now that provided the kernel is doing its job correctly, pseudo-concurrency and true concurrency will be indistinguishable at the concurrent programming level.

Since we assume that real concurrency and pseudo-concurrency are indistinguishable at this level, the reader may be wondering why the two terms have been introduced. In fact, it is sometimes assumed that the fact that there is only one processor being shared amongst all the processes makes the problems of controlling the interaction easier. That may be so in some instances, but we hope to show that the simple method of preventing interference, namely preventing the processor from being multiplexed, is not the best solution in many cases, and that by regarding pseudo-concurrency as being indistinguishable from real concurrency, general, and usually more satisfactory solutions to the problems of concurrent programming can result.

1.6   A Short History of Concurrent Programming

It is often assumed that Dijkstra instigated the study of concurrent programming in his now classic article "Co-operating Sequential Processes", published in 1967. Certainly in that article we see the introduction of some now well-known problems such as "The

Dining Philosophers", "The Sleeping Barber" and "The Dutch Flag Problem", and perhaps most importantly, the *critical section problem* and its solution using *semaphores*. This article was indeed the first to take a "high-level" view of concurrent programming. As an aside, it is interesting to note that the same article introduces the notion of *deadlock*, and presents an algorithm which can detect the possible presence of deadlocks.

However, a more machine-language-oriented approach to concurrency was presented in the early 1960's, first by Conway and then by Dennis and Van Horn. The idea of multiple threads of control was introduced at this time, and it is interesting to observe that some of the problems of accessing shared resources such as memory were also addressed at that time.

As in the development of high-level (sequential) programming languages, researchers came to realise the problems associated with using these low-level constructs, mainly in the area of trying to write programs correctly and quickly, and as a result higher-level and more restrictive constructs were invented. Thus we now see a plethora of different techniques for providing controlled concurrent programming, many of which we shall be examining in greater detail in the later chapters of this book.

1.7   A Map of the Book

We shall examine the fundamental structures of concurrent programming in the following chapter, showing how concurrent activity may be specified and introducing the principal components from which concurrent programs are constructed. This will include a more formal definition of the notion of a process than that given earlier in this chapter, and we shall also examine more closely the ways in which processes may be created and destroyed. In chapter 3, we shall deal in greater depth with the problems of interaction between processes, showing how control of such interactions can be achieved with only the minimum of assistance from the hardware, while at the same time demonstrating that some hardware assistance is necessary. From these small beginnings, we shall build up a whole hierarchy of concurrency control techniques. At an appropriate stage, we shall call for help on slightly more functionality in the hardware. This chapter deals with the lowest level of interaction which is concerned with the non-interference of processes at critical points in their respective executions. At a higher level, we shall be interested not only in the problem of non-interference of processes, but also in the positive interaction between them. A number of high level constructs for communication between concurrent processes have been proposed, and these will be dealt with in chapters 4 and 5.

In describing these higher-level programming structures for the control of concurrency, we will show how such structures provide more natural ways in which to express the solutions to concurrency problems, in much the same way as high-level programming languages provide a more natural way of solving ordinary sequential programming problems than can be achieved using machine or assembly language. It is convenient to classify the type of interaction which takes place between concurrent processes into two classes; shared data and message passing. In the former case, a process is permitted to access data which is also accessible by one or more simultaneously active processes. We shall see that difficulties can be introduced by unconstrained simultaneous access to shared data, and chapter 4 discusses methods by which such problems can be avoided. In chapter 5, we examine various methods and mechanisms for passing information between processes without the necessity for allowing explicit access to a shared resource. In chapter 6, we illustrate some of the principles by discussing various solutions to a particular problem in concurrent programming, using a number of concurrent languages which are presently available.

Finally, in chapter 7, we give some indications of how some of the concurrency structures introduced in the earlier chapters may be implemented, including the construction of a multiplexing kernel to provide the illusion of multiple processors.

1.8 Exercises

1.1 Draw the tree which represents the evaluation of the arithmetic expression:

$$(a ** 2 + (c + d) * e) + (f + g * h)$$

How many operations does this evaluation require?

1.2 Assuming that access to a variable or constant is instantaneous, and that each operation takes one unit of time, how many units of time would 'e required to evaluate the expression given in exercise 1.1

(a). sequentially,

(b). concurrently, as defined by the tree structure (assuming that sufficient processors are available to allow maximal concurrency).

1.3 Repeat exercise 1.2, given that the time taken by each operation is:

    + -   1 unit
    * -   2 units
    ** -   4 units.

1.4 Given the following Pascal program:

```
          program SimpleArithmetic;
          var a, b, sum, diff : integer;
          begin
(A)           a := 25;
(B)           b := 17;
(C)           sum := a + b;
(D)           diff := a - b;
          end; { SimpleArithmetic }
```

construct a partial ordering on the statements of the program (labelled A, B, C and D at the left hand side of each executable statement).

1.5   For the program given in exercise 1.4, and using the partial ordering found, draw the corresponding acyclic graph.

1.6   In the following Pascal program, label the various iterations of the **for** statements in a suitable way (for example, by the letters $A_1, A_2, \ldots A_5, D_1, D_2, \ldots D_5$)and hence show the extent to which this program may also be made concurrent:

```
        program Fibonacci;
        var i : 1..5;
            A : array [1..5] of integer;
            F : array [0..6] of integer;
        begin
(A)         for i := 1 to 5 do A[i] := 0;
(B)         F[0] := 0;
(C)         F[1] := 1;
(D)         for i := 1 to 5 do F[i+1] := F[i-1] + F[i];
        end; { Fibonacci }
```

1.7   Examine the component actions in an everyday task such as preparing a meal. How much concurrency is there already? To what extent could additional concurrency be introduced if there were two (or more) people involved instead of one? Where do conflicts arise? What constraints are there which prohibit the introduction of concurrent activity?

2
Processes and the Specification of Concurrency

In the previous chapter we introduced the notion of a sequential process (agreeing that where no confusion would arise, the term *process* would be sufficient) in an informal way. Now we need to formalise this concept, and to provide some concrete examples of the representation of a process which will enable us to clarify the basic ideas behind systems of concurrent processes. We begin, however, by considering some of the issues concerning the nature of concurrent activity, and describing some of the notations which have been proposed whereby concurrency may be introduced into a program.

2.1 Specification of Concurrent Activity

There are a variety of ways of talking about concurrency, some of which have found their way into programming languages in various guises, and some of which are merely notational mechanisms for describing parallel activity.

When discussing the ways in which parallel activity can be specified within a programming language or system, it is useful to consider two orthogonal features of any proposed method. The first is the specification of where in a program a separate process may be started, and where, if at all, it terminates. The specification of where a new process may begin and end provides some *synchronisation points* within the concurrent program. We assume that it is possible to specify that two processes may execute in parallel, and it is at that point that the two processes are assumed to be synchronised. After this point, the two processes proceed at their own rates, and no further assumptions may be made about the point each has reached in its execution relative to the other. Only when they are required to resynchronise with each other can anything more be said about the relationship between the timings of the processes. This issue we shall refer to as *flexibility*. Some parallel systems are very restrictive in where processes may begin and end, often to the point where all processes must begin together at the start of the concurrent program, and only end when the whole program completes, while others will allow new processes to be started at any time, and to terminate (and resynchronise) at any time.

The second issue that may be considered in relation to the specification of concurrent activity is that of *granularity*. This is concerned with the size of unit of executable code which may be specified as comprising a separate process. The granularity of the concurrent activity may be as small as a single machine instruction, or as large as a complete program. Clearly, the ability to specify that two or more machine instructions are to be executed in parallel allows the maximum degree of parallelism to be introduced into a program, and would be necessary in, for example, the parallel computations required in the evaluation of an arithmetic expression (as in figure 1.1 in chapter 1). On the other hand, if the creation of a new process implied a call to the operating system to allocate space in which the process may run, then creating a new process for each new machine instruction would be both inefficient and prohibitively expensive.

A fairly common compromise in many programming languages which support concurrent programming is to allow processes to be created of the size of a procedure. This appears to be an acceptable compromise between the efficiency/expense requirement and the desire for maximum parallelism. However, especially in some of the notations whose primary purpose is descriptive rather than implementable, granularity at the level of the program statement (e.g. the Pascal statement) is often permissible.

2.2   Threads of Control

Some of the earliest work in concurrent programming was described by Conway and by Dennis and Van Horn. This work concerned itself with the "threads of control" approach to processes, examining the ways in which multiple threads of execution could be specified. Such was the lack of development of high-level programming languages at this time, that the descriptions are couched in terms of machine or assembly-language constructs. It is in this work that the terms *fork* and *join* first appear. The origin of these terms is clearly derived from flowchart representations of programs, in which the beginning of separate threads of execution within the program would appear as a branch or fork in the diagram, and the recombining of two (or more) threads would be represented by a point in the flowchart at which two paths join again.

The first proposal which described the *fork* construct assumed that a machine instruction of that name existed. If a machine language program encounters a conditional branch instruction such as:

> BZ   *a*
> *b*:...

we would expect this to be interpreted as an instruction to examine a condition code, and to cause execution to continue at *a* if the condition code indicated that a zero result flag was set, and at *b* otherwise; i.e. execution would continue *either* at *a* or at *b* according to the condition code. Conway proposed the provision of a machine instruction:

> FORK   *a*
> *b*:...

which causes the thread of execution to divide, and the program continues *both* at *a* and at *b* simultaneously. In the conditional branch example, the threads of control will (usually) meet again at some point in the program after executing only one of the two possible sequences of instructions. In the case of the *fork*, two parallel threads of execution have been created, and it must be possible to recombine them into a single thread again at a suitable point. This is achieved by using a

> JOIN *x*

machine instruction at the end of each separate execution path. The intention is that only the *join* at the end of the last execution path to terminate is effective in transferring control to *x*; the earlier path(s) merely terminate(s). The last path to complete can of course only be determined at run time, and indeed may be different on different occasions on which the program is run, hence the reason for the special *join* instruction. An implementation of this is proposed which involves the introduction of a counter to indicate how many separate execution paths are in existence following a fork or series of forks, and each join decrements this counter. Only the join which causes the counter to be decremented to zero actually causes control to pass to x.

The *fork* sets up a separate thread of execution, the code for which is stored at the address designated in the fork instruction, while at the same time, the original thread of execution continues uninterrupted. In this sense, and only in this sense, the new thread of control is inferior to the original thread of control, but for reasons related to subsequent refinements of the fork/join mechanism, we shall refer to the new thread of control as being the *child*, and the original as the *parent*. Figures 2.1(a) and (b) are intended to illustrate

Figure 2.1(a)

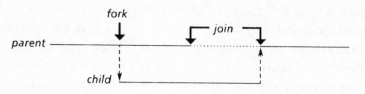

diagrammatically the action of fork and join. In figure 2.1(a), the *fork* creates the child, and the parent continues along its normal execution path until it reaches the *join*. Because the child has not yet completed its execution, i.e. in terms of the original proposal it has not yet reached its *join* instruction, the parent has to wait (or merely terminate), and the child is responsible for causing execution to resume correctly at the end of its code. Figure 2.1(b) illustrates the alternative situation where the child reaches its *join* first and simply

Figure 2.1(b)

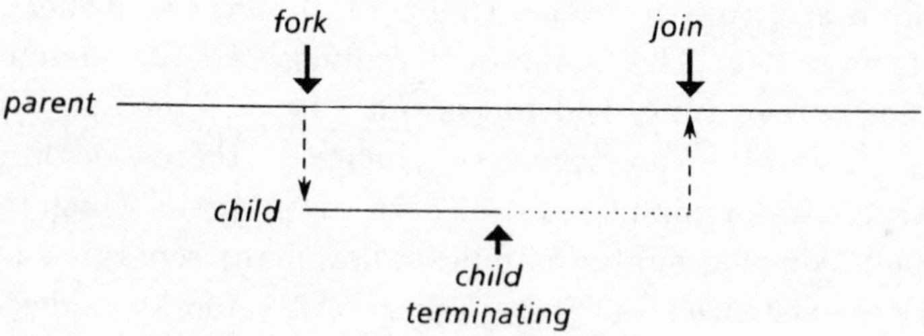

terminates, while the parent continues without delay at the point indicated by the *join*.

It would be a mistake to suggest that this early work concerned itself only with notions of threads of control, and in fact many of the concepts upon which much of present day concurrency control practice is based stem from this work. Concepts such as the state of a process, and the use of locking to control simultaneous access to shared resources are recognisable in these early reports. Such topics will be discussed at greater length in subsequent chapters.

2.3   Statement-Level Concurrency

The fundamental notion required to specify concurrency is to have some basic constructs which may be regarded as sequential in the ordinary programming language sense. In the previous section, the basic sequential construct was the usual sequential flow of control from one machine instruction to the next. Concurrency was introduced by allowing the possibility of two or more such threads proceeding in parallel. This could be described as instruction level concurrency, i.e. the granularity of the parallel activity could be at the level of the individual machine instruction. Furthermore, since the fork and join instructions may be used at any point in the program, this mechanism offers maximum flexibility. A slightly more structured view of concurrency could be taken by considering not the machine instruction level, but by considering a single high-level language statement to be the primitive construct.

2.3.1   Concurrent Statements

One of the earliest notations proposed was that of Dijkstra in his article "Co-operating Sequential Processes" in which the notation **parbegin** and **parend** (*parallel begin* and *parallel end*) was introduced. Since then a number of authors have used **cobegin** and **coend** (*concurrent begin* and *concurrent end*) to mean exactly the same thing.

This is the notation which we shall use, at least for the purposes of the examples in the following chapters, as it seems to us to be the clearest way to express concurrency in the simple examples which we shall be examining. As with the sequential **begin** and **end** as found in a language such as Pascal, the **cobegin** and **coend** are used to bracket a group of statements. Thus, we might expect to find that the definition of the language might include the BNF description:

<concurrent statement> :: =
    cobegin <statement list> coend

with <statement list> having the usual obvious meaning. Even in sequential programming, a statement list may have different interpretations depending upon the construct in which the list appears. In an ordinary block, however, we would expect each of the statements in the list to be executed in sequence, each one beginning to execute when its predecessor is complete, the whole statement being complete (i.e. the **end** being reached) when the last statement in the list has finished executing.

The action of the concurrent statement implies a certain synchronisation of concurrent activity, both when the concurrent statement begins, and when it is complete. All of the statements in the list associated with the concurrent statement must be thought of as beginning their execution at exactly the same instant of time. (In practice, this will only rarely be the case, but any delays in starting to execute any of the statements will be random and unpredictable, so that not only the precise moment at which each begins to execute will be impossible to determine, but so will the *order* in which the statements begin.) This operation is analogous with a *fork* being executed to initiate the execution of each statement in the list, except that a *fork* can only initiate one additional thread of control, and a sequence of *fork*s would determine the order in which the statements began their execution. The timing, and therefore the order, of the starting of each statement within the **cobegin/coend** block is arbitrary.

The **coend** has a role in the synchronisation mechanism too. If we assume that a concurrent statement might be included in a larger program, which would be the case if the concurrent statement should happen to be a part of a larger sequential activity, it will be necessary for the termination of the concurrent statement to be well defined. The semantics of the concurrent statement must include the requirement that the end of the statement occurs only when each of the members of the statement list has terminated. It is therefore necessary for the

coend to be aware of when each of the members of the statement list reaches the end of its action, and when it is recognised that they all have, then the concurrent statement can terminate, and the following statement in sequence may begin. This is of course equivalent to a *join* being executed at the end of each of the component statements.

This notation was first proposed by Dijkstra as a method of describing parallel or concurrent activity, but it was felt that in practice, the setting up and management of processes was a more extensive exercise than could be afforded, taking into account the rapidity with which processes would need to be created and destroyed, and the relatively little work that each would be required to do during its lifetime. In the light of subsequent developments mainly in hardware, such an approach has become more of a practical proposition, and languages have been designed and implemented which adopt this approach.

One such language is OCCAM†, which we discuss in more detail in a later chapter. However, the origins of OCCAM are worth exploring, and this is the subject of the next section.

The **cobegin/coend** structure is of course recursive, and the statements within the concurrent block may themselves be blocks (either sequential or concurrent). Thus it is often possible to take a partial order representation of the sequencing requirements of a program, as in section 1.3 and illustrated in figure 1.2, and create a concurrent program using the **cobegin/coend** notation. For instance, using the example of section 1.3, we may create the concurrent program shown as program 2.1. Since, however, the **cobegin/coend** notation requires a strict nesting of concurrent and sequential statements, there are instances which do not allow the direct translation from the acyclic graph notation of section 1.3 to the concurrent block notation.

2.3.2 Guarded Commands

Dijkstra (again!) was responsible for these concepts, when he discussed a construct called the *guarded command*. The original purpose of the guarded command was to attempt to provide a

---

†OCCAM is a trademark of Inmos Ltd.

```
begin
    A;
    cobegin
        B;
        begin
            cobegin
                C; D
            coend;
            E
        end
    coend;
    F;
    cobegin
        begin
            G; I
        end;
        begin
            H; J
        end
    coend
end
```

Program 2.1

framework for reasoning about non-determinism within programs. The specific example which Dijkstra was considering at the time he invented guarded commands was the problem of finding the greatest common divisor of two positive integers using Euclid's algorithm.

Euclid's algorithm is based on the observation that the greatest common divisor, $gcd(x, y)$, of two positive integers x and y is given by:

$$gcd(x,y) = \text{if } x = y \text{ then } x \text{ else}$$
$$\text{if } x > y \text{ then } gcd(x\text{-}y, y) \text{ else } gcd(x, y\text{-}x)$$

The algorithm which results is given (in a Pascal-like notation) as program 2.2. Dijkstra's concern was the lack of an elegant and consistent notation for the **if** statement within the loop.

The guarded command consists of a command (very much like a program statement), preceded by a Boolean expression, known as a *guard*. The rules of execution of a guarded command state that the command can only be executed if the Boolean expression evaluates to *true*. As an isolated entity, the guarded command is really no more than an **if** statement in a conventional programming language.

```
gcd := x:
while x < > y do
begin
    if x > y then x := x - y
    else { y > x } y := y - x;
    gcd := x
end;
```

Program 2.2

Guarded commands become a powerful tool only when they are combined together using the *alternative* construct and the *repetitive* construct.

The alternative construct introduces the non-determinacy by allowing a number of guarded commands to be grouped together, and allowing any one of the statements to be executed, provided its guard evaluates to *true*. Only one of the statements is executed, and in this sense the construct appears to be similar to a **case** statement in many conventional programming languages. The non-determinacy comes about because it is not essential that only one of the guards is true at a time, such as is the case in ADA for example, and there is no algorithmic rule which determines which statement (or command) should be executed (such as in the Mesa SELECT statement or the **switch** statement of the C programming language, in which the "guards" or selectors are scanned in lexical order within the program text until a *true* value is found).

To exemplify the alternative construct in a very simple way, consider the problem of assigning to a variable m the value of the larger of two variables x and y. In a conventional programming language notation, one might write:

if $x > y$ **then** $m := x$ **else** $m := y$;

This will obviously give the correct answer, but there is a slight asymmetry in this solution due to the fact that we actually have three separate relations between x and y to consider, namely $x > y$, $x < y$ and $x = y$. In this instance, we would of course argue that it does not matter whether we test for $x > y$ or $x \geq y$, since the result will be the same. However, the guarded command notation allows us to write down a symmetric solution, and allow a non-deterministic choice during the actual execution of the program to decide which statement will actually be used to assign the correct value to m. In the program, shown in program 2.3, **if** and **fi** delimit the alternative construct, the

> **if**
> $\quad x \geq y \to m := x$
> $\square$
> $\quad y \geq x \to m := y$
> **fi**

Program 2.3

symbol $\to$ separates the guard from the command, and the symbol $\square$ is used to separate the component guarded commands from each other. This solution clearly displays the inherent symmetry of the problem, but at the cost of the non-determinism which is introduced.

Returning to the problem of the greatest common divisor, use is made here of the repetitive construct to specify the looping within the algorithm. This construct is delimited by the symbols **do** and **od**, with the other symbols having the same meanings as before. The repetitive construct operates (as the name would suggest) by cycling around the component guarded commands, terminating only when all the guards are false. Thus, as we see in program 2.4, the loop will

> **do**
> $\quad x > y \to x := x - y$
> $\square$
> $\quad y > x \to y := y - x$
> **od**

Program 2.4

continue for as long as the values of x and y are different. The final value of x (or y) is obviously the required value for the greatest common divisor.

Comparing these guarded commands with the **cobegin/coend** notation of the previous section, we can see that the non-determinacy of the guarded commands is also present in the concurrent statement notation, but without the control provided by the guards. Dijkstra makes the point in his discussion of guarded commands that the commands which lie between **if** and **fi**, or between **do** and **od**, are an unordered set of guarded commands, in the sense that the lexical order in which they are written is immaterial, and the same remark could be made about the individual statements within the **cobegin/coend** construction.

2.3.3 CSP and OCCAM

Concurrency is not explicitly mentioned in the original discussion of guarded commands, but since the most obvious means by which non-determinacy can be introduced into a program is through parallelism, it became clear that guarded commands would be intimately related to concurrent structures, and eventually incorporated into languages which support concurrent programming.

The guarded command idea was extended by Hoare in his language CSP (Communicating Sequential Processes) by allowing the guards to become dependent upon the behaviour of another component of the program. We shall be dealing in the following chapters with the subject of inter-process co-operation and communication, suffice it to say here that the introduction of such notions puts the topic of guarded commands firmly into the area of concurrent programming, since the extended guards of CSP require the presence of another parallel activity to allow such guards to succeed.

A simplified form of the guarded command was incorporated into the language OCCAM, which we shall be discussing at greater length in chapter 6.

2.4 Procedure-Level Concurrency

The earliest high-level programming languages to incorporate concurrency features tended to be very concerned about the efficiency of process creation and destruction. To this end, processes were regarded as somewhat larger units than a simple statement, and usually they were created as the program began to run, and remained in existence until the program was halted. Some variation within this basic notion is possible, and in some languages the process is regarded as beginning to run as soon as it is defined, whereas in others the definition of a process is to be thought of in the same way as a type definition, where processes do not actually come into existence until a declaration is made of a variable of the "type". Even in this case, there can be variations based on whether the process (variable) begins its execution as soon as it is declared, or whether it only begins by explicit action of the program in the form of an **init** (or similar) statement.

To give some examples of languages offering such features, the language Concurrent Euclid allows the programmer to specify the definition of a **process**. A process definition looks very similar to a procedure declaration, except that there are restrictions upon where in the program such a definition may appear. The process definition has the effect not only of defining the action to be taken by the process, but also of initiating that action at the same time. The consequence of this approach is that only one process is created per process definition, and if it is required to initiate multiple versions of the same process, multiple process definitions must be supplied. This is not so much of a disadvantage as it might at first appear, because different processes may call a common procedure, but nevertheless it is sometimes inconvenient to have to provide separate definitions for two (or more) identical objects.

A number of languages based on Pascal, among them Pascal Plus, designed by a group at Queen's University, Belfast, and the language Pascal-m from Queen Mary College, London, give the programmer the facility of declaring objects of **type** *process*, and then allowing the declaration of *instances* or "variables" of this type. The type definition construct gives the specification of the actions to be taken by the process, but it is the declaration of the process instances which initiates the execution of a process as an independent concurrent entity. This approach does remove the problem created by the Concurrent Euclid style of process definition, in that multiple instances of identical processes may be initiated simply by declaring multiple instances of the same type. It is necessary, however, for the process instances to perform *identical* actions (although it is possible in Pascal-m, for example, for the instantiation of a process to take parameters which can alter the behaviour of the process).

One of the earliest languages to offer concurrency facilities was Concurrent Pascal, designed by Brinch Hansen in the early 1970's. This language permits the programmer to define a **type** *process*, and then to declare instances of the type. However, an additional **init** statement is required in order to start the execution of the process. This makes it possible for the various invocations of a process to be parameterised, providing the possibility of processes using the same algorithm(s) to operate upon different initial data.

In each of these three examples, we observe that the granularity of the concurrency is at the level of the procedure, but each example has more flexibility than the previous one. In Concurrent Euclid, all of the component processes are started at the beginning of the program, and run until they terminate. In Pascal Plus, the declaration of the process instance causes the execution of the process to begin, and thus a process may be started at any time when a new block of the program is entered. Finally, in Concurrent Pascal, the execution of a process may be started at any time, since the **init** statement may appear at any point in the program.

In none of these languages are there any facilities for the processes to resynchronise once they have been initiated. All of the languages provide for some kind of inter-process communication, and this will be considered in chapters 3, 4 and 5, but there is no provision for the multiple threads of control represented by the processes to come together again. In other words, they provide the equivalent of a *fork*, but not the equivalent of a *join*.

The final example of a language which supports procedure level concurrency, and which uses *fork* and *join* to implement it, is the programming language Mesa. Mesa was designed at the Xerox Corporation's Palo Alto Research Center as a language for developing large systems. It was realised during the course of the design of the language that some features for concurrency would need to be incorporated, and it was decided that a version of *fork* and *join* would be used. It has to be pointed out that the language also had other design aims, one of which was strong type-checking. The resultant mechanism for introducing concurrency therefore requires that type checking can be performed across calls of the concurrency constructs. This explains some of the restrictions which appear in the constructs. We present the examples using the Mesa syntax itself, on the assumption that this will be sufficiently similar to Pascal that it can be easily understood.

The specification of the code that a new process will be required to run is not dissimilar to the specification of the execution of a separate piece of code when a procedure is called. In fact, Mesa takes the view that a procedure may be declared in the standard way, and may then be executed either as a procedure, i.e. synchronously by suspending the execution of the calling program until the procedure returns, or else concurrently with the calling (or parent) process. Procedures are declared in Mesa as in the following example:

ProcName: **PROCEDURE** [*ParamType*]
RETURNS [*ResultType*] = ...

where the ellipsis represents the body of the procedure. We also assume that *ParamType* and *ResultType* have been suitably defined, and it should be pointed out that either of these may be empty, that is, the procedure may take no parameters and/or it may return no results. In the normal execution of a (sequential) process, a program may call the procedure *ProcName* in the usual way, i.e. by a statement such as:

res ← *ProcName* [*pars*];

As one would expect, the action of this statement is to suspend the execution of the calling program, pass control to the procedure *ProcName*, and resume execution of the caller when the procedure is finished. (We assume that there are appropriate declarations of the variables *pars* and *res*, which have types *ParamType* and *ResultType* respectively.) Note that this construct can be strongly type-checked, in that a compiler can ensure that the type of the parameters passed to the procedure agrees with the type expected by the procedure in its declaration, and similarly, the result returned by the procedure is assigned to a variable of the correct type.

The creation of an independent concurrent process can be achieved by using the **FORK** statement, and in order to inform the newly created process of the code it is to execute, the name of a procedure is supplied as an argument of the *fork*. For the purposes of resynchronisation later, it is necessary to declare a variable of an appropriate type which will take the value of the process's identity after it has been created. Thus, we first require a declaration such as:

pid: **PROCESS RETURNS** [*ResultType*];

Notice that, because of Mesa's requirement for strong type-checking, this declaration requires a specification not only that *pid* is to take a value representing a process, but also that the type of the value to be returned by the process is specified. We now can give the statement which actually invokes a new process:

pid ← FORK *ProcName* [*pars*];

As a result of this statement, the procedure *ProcName* begins to execute, and to use the parameters *pars*, but the process in which the FORK statement appears (i.e. the parent) also continues to run concurrently. The resynchronisation of the parent and child processes is achieved using the JOIN statement, which in this case might be:

res ← JOIN *pid*;

We observe that in this case, the process identifier *pid* is supplied as an argument to the JOIN construct, rather than being returned as a result. The implication of this is that the parent process must know, at the time the code is written, which process is to be JOINed. It is clear that this is the only way to allow the construct to work if the strong type-checking feature is to be preserved. It is not however, as much of a handicap as might at first appear. Suppose a process has FORKed several processes. It will require the same number of JOIN statements in order to resynchronise them all. The order in which these JOIN statements are written down will not matter, since each child process will only terminate when it both reaches the end of its own code, and when the parent reaches the JOIN for that particular process. It will not be concerned therefore if it has to wait for a little time longer until its parent is ready to JOIN with it. The only circumstance when some difficulty might arise is when the parent wishes to continue execution after JOINing with some, but not all, of the child processes it has created, and furthermore does not care which processes they are. This would appear to be a relatively rare occurrence, although it would be possible to invent a somewhat artificial example in which such a feature might be required.

The identification of processes with high-level language constructs such as procedures, moves us away from a purely "thread of control" approach to concurrent processes, since in most high-level languages, the invocation of a new procedure also implies the creation of additional variables, local to the newly invoked procedure. It is therefore no longer sufficient to think of multiple processes as merely additional flows of control - multiple program counters, perhaps - but we now have to consider there being storage associated with each new process. This leads to a completely fresh view of a process in which not only must the code to be executed be specified at the time of creating a new process, but also a region of memory must be identified as being associated with the process, and this we might refer to as the *address space* of the process. For example, when a sequential program written in a high-level language such as Pascal is running, at any moment of time it is possible to identify those variables which the program is capable of accessing. If this program calls another procedure, some of these variables will become inaccessible, while a new set of variables will be added to the set of visible variables. We may describe the address space of a program as being those variables which are accessible by the program at any particular moment of time. We can see that the address space of a program will vary as the execution of the program proceeds.

When multiple concurrent processes are involved, it is clear that each process will also have a particular set of variables which it can access, some of which may be accessible to other processes as well. We may still refer to the set of variables accessible to a process as its address space, but we now have to recognise that each process will have a different address space. It may also be that two address spaces may overlap, and the corresponding processes may have access to a set of variables common to both. The problems associated with processes having overlapping address spaces - the so-called shared memory problem - are covered in detail in the next two chapters, but we do need at this point to observe that our notion of a sequential process must acknowledge that the description of a process has to include both the code it executes and the address space within which it has to operate.

2.5   Program-Level Concurrency

Every operating system which has any facilities for providing simultaneous interactive access to multiple users, or for processing multiple parallel streams of jobs, must be able to handle a set of concurrent processes. Even if the system has a totally static structure in which no additional processes are created and no processes are destroyed during the life of the system, concurrent processing will require some kind of view of what a process is. In the simplest possible case, there must at least be one process to look after each of the interactive terminals, even if the invocation of a program by a user causes that process to "call" the program as a procedure. Other systems may take the view that the creation of a new process is required whenever a user wishes to start a new program executing. The creator of the new process may or may not be suspended until the new process terminates. In such systems, it may be said that the granularity of concurrency is the whole program.

Concurrency within the UNIX† operating system has the granularity of a whole program, and it uses this latter technique to execute programs and commands at the request of the user, although the user may specify whether the parent process is to regain control immediately or to wait until the child process terminates. User programs may, however, create new processes for their own purposes, although they may still only execute whole programs within a process.

When UNIX is asked to create a new process, it creates an identical copy (a "clone") of the process which requested the new process. That is, a process may request the creation of a new process by calling the system call *fork* as in:

$$pid := fork;$$

where *pid* is a variable which receives the identity of the newly created process. It is not our intention to describe all of the subtleties of the UNIX *fork* call, suffice it to say that the "cloned" process is an identical copy of the code and data of the parent process with one exception. That is that the value of *pid* only contains the identity of the newly created process in the data space of the parent, whereas the value of *pid* within the child process is zero. Using this knowledge, the process can determine whether it is executing code in the child or in the parent.

---

†UNIX is a trademark of AT&T Laboratories

At first sight, this mechanism would not appear to be very useful, but the *fork* system call is usually used in conjunction with another system call called *exec*. The function of the *exec* call is to fetch a new program from the file system, and to overlay the running program with the new one. Any process calling *exec* is intentionally destroying itself, and replacing itself with an entirely new program. In conjunction with the *fork* call, therefore, it is possible to create an identical copy of a process, to determine which copy is the clone, and to overlay the clone with a new program, leaving the original parent process to run the original program.

This is the mechanism by which processes begin a new existence, together with the *exec* call which provides them with code to run, and of course a new address space (initially) identical to the parent's is also made available, but UNIX also provides a mechanism by which processes can resynchronise themselves. This is essentially the *join* construct, but in fact in UNIX it is implemented using the *wait* system call.

When a parent process reaches the point where it cannot continue unless it knows that a particular child process has terminated, it calls the *wait* system call. This indicates that the execution of the parent must be suspended until the child is known to have terminated. If this event has already occurred, then the parent is not delayed, but if the parent reaches the *wait* call first, then it must be delayed until the child code reaches its *exit* call. The fragment of code given in program 2.5 illustrates the mechanism. We do not discuss here the problem of how the two processes might pass data to one another; the topic of inter-process communication is left until later in the book.

In detail, we see in program 2.5 that following the call of *fork*, a test is made of the value of the variable *pid*. If this value is zero, then the code executing is the child's code, which will generally need to be replaced by a new program. The ellipsis before the *exec* call which performs the overlaying is intended to indicate that some code could be provided which ensures that any inter-process communication mechanisms which may be required are set up correctly before the *exec* call is made. As the following comment points out, the action of the *exec* system call implies that any code after the call will only be executed if the *exec* fails for any reason.

```
pid := fork;
if pid = 0 then
begin
      { this is code executed by the child process      }
      ...
      exec (...);
      { provided the exec call was successful,           }
      { this point is never reached, as this process     }
      { has now been overlayed by a new program          }
end else
begin
      { this is the parent }
      ...
      cpid := wait (s);
      { presumably cpid = pid at this point      }
      ...
end
```

Program 2.5

The child will supply a status value when it reaches an *exit* statement, and it may be desirable for the parent to discover this status value as part of the resynchronisation. It may be necessary, for instance, for the parent to know whether the child successfully completed its task. This is the purpose of the parameter of the *wait* system call, which provides a **var** parameter *s* to the *wait* call in which the exit status may be returned. The returned value of the call itself is the identifier of the process which has terminated. It can be seen from this that if a parent has created several child processes, the *wait* call will be satisfied, and the parent process allowed to continue, when any of the child processes terminates, and the parent is able to discover the identity of the terminating process by the value returned by the *wait* call. If the parent needs to wait for a particular process to finish, then it will have to issue several *wait* calls, until the result returned indicates that the required process has indeed completed.

Summarising these two examples which employ *fork* and *join*, we observe that:

(a)   Both UNIX and Mesa will allow processes to be *fork*ed at any point in the code, making it an extremely flexible method. By the same token, they can execute *join* statements at (almost) any time. The difference here is that since the Mesa JOIN must specify the process to be joined, the process identifier must be in scope, and hence may limit the positions where the JOIN may occur.

(b)   UNIX requires that the code to be executed (which we assume will normally be placed in the memory using an *exec* call) should be loaded as a whole program, whereas Mesa regards the code of a process to be of the same granularity as a procedure. In fact, Mesa goes further and allows procedures declared in the program to be called as procedures in the ordinary way, or as processes, according to the wishes of the programmer.

(c)   Because of the requirement in Mesa that the program should be strongly type-checkable, the JOIN statement is slightly less flexible than the corresponding construct in UNIX. For most examples, however, we would expect that both constructs would be flexible enough.

(d)   Although we are not at this point concerned with the way in which independent processes interact with each other during their respective executions, we may also observe here that the Mesa model allows a forked process to access those variables which were in existence at the time the FORK call was made, and thus two (or more) processes can access the same resources. By contrast, in the UNIX model, the variables which had been declared at the time of the fork are copied to the child process, and two instances of each variable are now in existence, each process having access to only one of them. Inter-process communication in the UNIX form of concurrency is handled quite differently, as we shall see in chapter 5.

2.6   The Formal Model of a Process

The formal model of a process which we shall use was first introduced by Horning and Randell. We shall not attempt to describe this approach in all its full generality, but it may be helpful to consider the formal model in order to understand what is required to describe a process, particularly when an implementation of the process abstraction is required, as would be the case if a kernel to support pseudo-concurrency were being designed.

One of the informal definitions of a process given in the previous chapter was "that which runs on a processor". This of course begs the question of what is meant by a processor, but if we could provide a suitable definition of what "running on a processor" implies, then a concrete interpretation could be associated with the concepts of the formal model. For our purposes, a (sequential) processor consists of a device which is capable of accessing other devices (such as a memory) in order to retrieve information from, or send information to, that device. The characteristics of the target device are of no concern at present. The processor may also possess its own internal storage which can hold information. Most importantly, the processor encapsulates an algorithm by which it can always determine what *action* it must perform next (assuming it is not halted). The so-called *fetch/execute* cycle of a processor is a well-defined procedure which retrieves information from a memory at an address indicated by one of its internal registers (usually called the *program counter* or *pc*). The information thus retrieved is stored in another of the processor's private registers (often called the *instruction buffer*), after which it will be used by the processor to determine what its next action should be. This subsequent action may well cause other changes to take place within the processor's private storage, and may also involve interaction with other devices. Certainly, it would be expected that the value of *pc* would change as a result of the execution of each instruction, but the complete action will depend on the data retrieved and the Principles of Operation of the processor. When each instruction is complete, the processor will begin its fetch/execute cycle again, but this time with a (presumably) different value for *pc*.

The formal model describes a process in terms of a set of *state variables*. At any given moment of time, each of the state variables will contain a particular value, and this collection of values is known as the *state* of the process. The behaviour of a process can be described in terms of an *action function* which is a mapping from one state to another. Thus a process will begin in an initial state, and through successive applications of the action function will move through a sequence of states in order to carry out the required *computation*. Notice that the actions taken are entirely dependent upon the state of the processor at the time the action function is applied.

The action function is completely determined by the design of the hardware (or the firmware/software interpreter) on which the process is running, and it is the state of the process which concerns us here. Because we are concerned with the possible interactions of processes which may be running concurrently, we need to be able to consider the states of the various concurrently active processes, and the interrelationships of those states. As we shall see in later chapters, we will consider the interrelationships as falling into two categories - one in which some values from the state of one process are used to modify the state of another, and one in which the state spaces of two (or more) processes actually overlap, i.e. the two sets of state variables have a non-empty intersection.

In chapter 7, we shall consider the problem of implementing pseudo-concurrency, and in so doing, we will need to consider what would happen if we should wish to suspend the actions of a process at any arbitrary moment in time. We clearly would like to be sure that a suspended process could resume its execution as though it had never been interrupted. If a processor is only concerned with the execution of a single process, then provided that the action of halting the processor does not lose any information, restarting the processor should cause the process to continue to run. If however, the processor should be required to perform some other function between the suspension of a process's execution and its resumption, then the information held within the processor will almost certainly have been altered, in which case it will be necessary to record the state of the process at the moment of suspension - i.e. to take a *snapshot* of the process - so that when the process is resumed, the state can be re-established in order that the process may continue as though no suspension had taken place.

A process may, at any time during its execution, make use of any of the values which it may access, whether they be processor registers, memory locations, or whatever. It follows, therefore, that the state of a process must include all such values, and all these values must be preserved during the period when the processor is doing work on behalf of another process. This represents a very large state space, and the security of the information held in it by writing it to some secure storage would normally be prohibitively expensive to implement. Fortunately, however, we are usually able to partition the state space into a region which must be re-used by another process, and a region which may be regarded as private to a process for the duration of the existence of the process, irrespective of whether or not the process is making progress or not.

It is usually the case that the former region is very much smaller than the latter, which makes it practicable to consider saving that region in secure storage when the process is suspended, and restoring it when the process is ready to make further progress.

2.7 Examples of Process States

Two examples, one from a real computer and one from a conceptual high-level language machine (which has in fact a real implementation) will help to illustrate this idea of process state. This second example will appear again in chapter 7, when we describe the implementation of a concurrency kernel for a single processor computer.

2.7.1 Motorola M68000 Processor

Consider first a Motorola M68000 processor chip. Basically, this processor consists of sixteen "general purpose" registers, eight "data" registers designated $d0$ to $d7$, and eight "address" registers called $a0$ to $a7$. In addition, the processor contains a *program counter* (*pc*) and a register called the *processor status word* (or *p.s.w.*). The program counter contains the address in memory of the next instruction to be fetched, and the p.s.w. contains information about the internal status of the processor, such as the condition codes, which give some indication of the result of the last instruction executed. The p.s.w. may have some bearing on the subsequent behaviour of the processor. The state of a process running on such a machine, therefore, might be thought to be the whole of the memory accessible to the processor, together with the general purpose registers, the pc, and the p.s.w. It is this state which constitutes the required snapshot of a process if it is desired to save the state of the process in such a way that it can be restarted on a later occasion. More complex systems using the M68000 processor may contain additional components which would also need to be regarded as part of the state; for example, floating-point registers or hardware memory address translation registers.

2.7.2   A Hypothetical Pascal Processor

As our second example, we consider a hypothetical stack-based machine designed to run Pascal programs. The memory of the machine consists of two regions, one containing the program code and one in which the data is held, as shown in figure 2.2. Conceptually, the

Figure 2.2

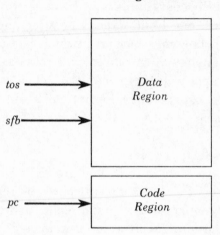

machine executes Pascal statements taken from the code region, and operates on program variables whose values are stored in the data region. All variables are referred to by the program in terms of offsets from one of two pointers into the data stack. Each procedure within the Pascal program (including the main program) uses its own *stack frame* within the data region to hold its parameters, its local variables and its working space. When a new procedure is called, a new stack frame is created on the top of the stack which contains, in addition to the local data of the new procedure, linkage information allowing non-local data to be accessed, and also the necessary information to allow the stack to be restored to its former state on exit from the procedure. For this particular architecture, we see that the state of a process running on this hypothetical machine consists firstly of the two regions of memory, and also of the three pointers into the memory shown in figure 2.2, the program counter *pc*, (which of course indicates the position in the code region where the next Pascal statement to be executed will be found), a base pointer for the current stack frame *sfb*, and a pointer to the top of the stack *tos*. If a snapshot of a process running within such an architecture were required, it would need to consist of the contents of both regions of memory, together with the values of *pc*, *sfb* and *tos*. (It will be noticed that we have considered only the data storage which is organised as a stack, and ignored the facilities for allocating and de-allocating memory explicitly from a heap region. Since the use of storage organised in this way introduces issues such as the validity of pointer variables, we have chosen to ignore such matters for the time being, and we assume that our Pascal machine does not include support for the dynamic storage allocation and de-allocation, including the operations *new* and *dispose*. We claim that the inclusion of such facilities is easily accomplished if required, but for the purposes of this discussion will be omitted in the interests of clarity.)

The action of this machine consists of retrieving the Pascal statement indicated by *pc* from the code region and causing transformations on the data in the data region to occur according to the semantics of the Pascal language. As a result, *pc* will almost certainly change, and so possibly would *sfb* and *tos*.

The discussion in this section is intended to provide some formality to the rather vague notion of process introduced in chapter 1, and to provide a couple of concrete realisations of the formal model in order to try to give a clearer picture of what is meant by a process in the subsequent sections and chapters. Further consideration of states will not appear until the discussion of implementation in chapter 7. We shall however, be seeing examples of the various methods of specifying concurrent activity in the succeeding chapters.

2.8   Exercises

2.1   A program consists of nine statements represented by the letters A, B, C, D, E, F, G, H and I which must be executed according to the partial ordering:

$$A<C, B<C, C<D, C<E, D<G, D<F, F<H, E<I, G<I, H<I$$

Draw a directed graph which represents this partial ordering.

2.2   Write a concurrent program using the cobegin/coend notation which exploits all the concurrency possible given the constraints of the partial ordering given in exercise 2.1.

2.3   How does the directed graph of exercise 2.1, and the corresponding concurrent program of exercise 2.2 change if the following additional constraints are introduced?
(a) $D<H$.
(b) $E<F$.
(c) $H<C$.

2.4   If A, B and C are 3×3 (integer) matrices, the following procedure makes C into the matrix product $A\times B$.

```
procedure matmult (A, B : matrix; var C : matrix);
  var i, j, k : 1..3;
      sum : integer;
  begin
    for i := 1 to 3 do
    for j := 1 to 3 do
    begin
      sum := 0;
      for k := 1 to 3 do sum := sum + A[i,k] * B[k,j];
      C[i,j] := sum
    end
  end; { matmult }
```

Modify the procedure to introduce concurrency wherever possible.

2.5 The following recursive **procedure** encapsulates the basis of Hoare's *quicksort* method for sorting a list of numbers $a[1..N]$. The procedure *split* re-arranges the numbers, and returns a value m such that $a[i] <= a[m]$ for $i < m$, and $a[m] < a[i]$ for $i > m$.

```
procedure quicksort
    (var a : array [1..N] of integer; s, t : integer);
var m : integer;
begin
  if t > s then
  begin
    m := split (a, s, t);
    quicksort (a, s, m-1);
    quicksort (a, m+1, t)
  end
end; { quicksort }
```

Describe how concurrency may be introduced into the procedure, and hence rewrite the procedure using **cobegin/coend**.

2.6 In exercise 2.5, assuming that there are sufficient processors for each new concurrent activity to start immediately, identify the best and worst cases with respect to the time which the concurrent program would take to execute, given that the time taken for *split* to execute is proportional to $t - s$ (i.e. the size of the list being divided).

3
Communication between Processes

As long as all of the concurrent processes are proceeding completely independently of each other, we would expect them all to continue at their own speed until they terminate (if they do). If this does not happen, that is if the results of a process are affected by the presence or absence of another supposedly independent process, then we have to investigate the underlying mechanism to find the reason for this problem. For the purposes of the discussion of the concurrent processes themselves, they will have an effect on one another only if they are required to communicate with each other.

We have already seen one example of inter-process communication as manifested in one of the process creation and deletion methods. This entailed the parent process calling the *fork* operation to initiate the child process, and the subsequent *join* operation (if there is one) as a way of resynchronising the parent and child. These two operations are very restrictive, allowing as they do the parent and child to synchronise with each other only when the child begins and ends its execution. What is required is a more general mechanism (or mechanisms) by which two processes may communicate with each other, not just at the beginning and end of the lives of the processes. A discussion of several possible methods is the subject of this chapter.

3.1 Interference, Co-operation and Arbitrary Interleaving

If two processes wish to communicate with each other, then this implies that they need to share some common information. If this were not so, then the two processes would be totally independent of each other and could proceed in parallel without any interference between them. Thus some information or *resource*, is to be shared by two or more processes. Shared resources may be regions of memory or peripheral devices to which both processes require access. Sometimes, simultaneous access to a resource by more than one process is permissible, but more frequently it will be necessary to impose the restriction that only a limited number of processes (usually only one) can have access to the resource at any one time.

Let us consider communication between concurrent processes as having two guises, interference and co-operation. We shall generally regard interference as an occurrence in which one process is able to interfere with the progress, and more importantly, with the outcome or results of another process. On the other hand, we shall regard co-operation to be a generally desirable feature which only affects the behaviour of the participant processes in a constructive way, if at all.

Processes executing concurrently and independently may proceed at their own rate, and no assumptions may be made about the relative times at which they carry out their individual actions. Even with pseudo-concurrency, the primitive operations of each process may be executed at arbitrary moments in time with respect to the times at which other processes' primitive operations are carried out. It will be true, of course, that the primitive operations within each (sequential) process will be executed in the correct order, but those operations may be interleaved with the operations of other processes in a completely arbitrary way. In order to understand the behaviour of two or more interfering processes we must also be clear about what is meant by a "primitive operation" in the context of the executing processes. Two examples may illustrate the problem of the primitive operation and of arbitrary interleaving.

Example 1. -   Incrementation of a Shared Variable.

Suppose two processes *P1* and *P2* wish to increment the value of a shared variable *count* by 1. This may be represented by program 3.1.

If we assume that the incrementation of the variable is a primitive operation, this will cause no difficulty, and the variable *count* will be correctly incremented by 2 at the end of this concurrent statement. If, however, the

cobegin

> P1:   *count* := *count* + 1;
> P2:   *count* := *count* + 1

coend

Program 3.1

machine(s) on which these concurrent statements are to be run does not permit "atomic" incrementation of variables in memory, and that the value must be retrieved from memory to a register, incremented in a register and then restored in memory, it will be necessary to expand the concurrent program as shown by program 3.2 where each of the statements

cobegin

> P1:   **begin**
> > *reg1* := *count*;
> > *reg1* := *reg1* + 1;
> > *count* := *reg1*
>
> **end**;
>
> P2:   **begin**
> > *reg2* := *count*;
> > *reg2* := *reg2* + 1;
> > *count* := *reg2*
>
> **end**

coend

Program 3.2

appearing within the begin blocks are taken to be indivisible, and *reg1* and *reg2* are registers which may be incremented, and are private to *P1* and *P2* respectively. Under the arbitrary interleaving assumption, we could conceivably find that these statements are executed in the order suggested by program 3.3.

begin

> $reg1 := count;$
> $reg1 := reg1 + 1;$
> $reg2 := count;$
> $count := reg1;$
> $reg2 := reg2 + 1;$
> $count := reg2$

end

> **Program 3.3**

The constraint that within each process the operations must be carried out in the correct sequential order is satisfied for the two processes separately, but with this sequence of interleaved operations, the final value of *count* will only be 1 greater than its original value, whereas it should have been incremented by 2.

Example 2. - Access to a Shared Disk.

In this example, the processes *P1* and *P2* are attempting to use the same random access input/output device. Specifically, suppose *P1* attempts to read from block 20 of the device, and *P2*'s task is to write to block 88. We may write this as:

> **cobegin**
>
> > $P1:$ *read* (20);
> > $P2:$ *write* (88)
>
> **coend**

Once again, if reading and writing of blocks are indivisible operations, these two operations may take place without interference, but if what really happens is:

cobegin

P1: **begin**
        seek (20); *read*
    end;

P2: **begin**
        seek (88); *write*
    end

coend

then a possible interleaving would be:

seek (20); *seek* (88); *read; write*

which presumably *P2* would find acceptable, but *P1* would not! An even worse situation could arise if the operations occurred in the order:

seek (88); *seek* (20); *write; read*

In this case, neither *P1* nor *P2* would be satisfied with the outcome!

These two examples serve to show the undesirable aspect of interference, but they also suggest a method by which the problem may be overcome. What is required is some way in which a group or sequence of statements may be flagged as being indivisible or atomic when in reality they are not. The problem arises because a shared resource requires an operation to be applied to it, and that this operation cannot be carried out indivisibly. Thus the solution is to provide a mechanism whereby the operation can be protected from interference while it is in progress. This entails the provision of a mechanism whereby a process can signal to all other processes that access to the resource should be avoided for the time being.

3.2   The Critical Section Problem

Before proceeding to discuss a range of solutions to this problem, we shall introduce a canonical example of the situation which frequently arises in practice, and which will provide a framework within which to discuss possible solutions. It is the critical section problem of Dijkstra which may be described as in program 3.4.

```
cobegin
    P1:  repeat
             critical_section_1;
             non_critical_section_1
         until false;

    P2:  repeat
             critical_section_2;
             non_critical_section_2
         until false

coend
```

Program 3.4

We assume that the two processes *P1* and *P2* are both infinite loops, each alternating between a critical section and a non-critical section, an assumption which appears to be justified if the two processes are part of an operating system providing a continuous service to its users. The critical sections need not consist of the same set of operations; they merely access the same shared resource. The non-critical sections are considered to be totally independent of one another.

There are three ground rules that must be obeyed by any solution to the critical section problem:

1. No more than one process may be within its critical section at any one time.
2. No process which wishes to enter its critical section may be delayed indefinitely, irrespective of what may happen within the non-critical section of another process.
3. No assumptions may be made about the relative speeds of the processes.

(We have to make the assumption that no process stays in its critical section indefinitely, as this would probably have a disastrous effect on the whole set of processes. Rule 2 however admits the possibility of a process remaining in its non-critical section indefinitely, provided that such an occurrence does not affect other processes' behaviour.)

In Example 1, we demonstrated that a lack of atomicity, combined with an unfortunate interleaving of the operations of *P1* and *P2*, would cause the value of *count* to be 1 less than it ought to be. However we did assume that the separate operations of the two processes would be interleaved rather than happening truly concurrently. Suppose now that the two indivisible operations:

$$count := reg1 \qquad \{ \text{from } P1 \}$$

and:

$$count := reg2 \qquad \{ \text{from } P2 \}$$

were running on separate processors at precisely the same instant. What would we expect the value of the shared variable *count* to be then? The answer to this question is that we must have some arbitration at some level of the system, and for the purposes of the ensuing discussion we shall assume that the arbitration takes place at the hardware level, at the point where processors are writing values to and reading values from memory. If two processors are attempting to access the same memory location at the same instant, then the hardware invokes the *memory interlock* which ensures that only one access can succeed, and the other must wait. Thus if two simultaneous writes are attempted, one will succeed first, and the other will be allowed to continue only when the first has finished, so that the final value of the target memory location will be one or other of the two values presented, and not some arbitrary bit pattern formed by a combination of the two. Similarly, if one process was attempting to read from a memory location at the same time as another was trying to write to that location, either the read will succeed before the write, in which case the value read will be the old value held by the location, or else the write will be first to execute, in which case the read will retrieve the new value of the location. The memory interlock ensures that the read does not return some arbitrary partially formed value.

From the memory interlock, we shall show that more sophisticated mechanisms can be constructed in order to solve the critical section problem. Note that throughout the following discussion we shall assume that the granularity of the interleaving of statements will be at least as fine as a single Pascal statement, and probably finer (since Pascal statements in general will compile into more than one machine instruction, and we cannot guarantee that interleaving of machine instructions will not occur).

3.3   Solutions to the Critical Section Problem

As an initial attempt at a solution of the critical section problem, suppose that there are two shared variables *claim1* and

```
{ Solution 1 }
var claim1, claim2: Boolean;
begin
    claim1 := false; claim2 := false;

cobegin

    P1:    repeat
               repeat { do nothing } until not claim2;
               claim1 := true;
               critical__section__1;
               claim1 := false;
               non__critical__section__1
           until false;

    P2:    repeat
               repeat { do nothing } until not claim1;
               claim2 := true;
               critical__section__2;
               claim2 := false;
               non__critical__section__2
           until false

coend
end
```

Program 3.5

claim2 specifically to control the mutual exclusion of *P1* and *P2* from their critical sections, i.e. there will of course be the shared resources which the critical sections themselves are designed to protect, and *claim1* and *claim2* are additional shared variables solely for the purpose of implementing the critical section mechanism. They are used to make claims on the use of the critical section on behalf of *P1* and *P2* respectively. Thus the first attempt at a solution might be program 3.5.

It is fairly easy to see that if the two processes *P1* and *P2* were to proceed in perfect synchronisation, then both would arrive within their respective critical sections at the same time, thus violating ground rule 1, since both would see that the other has made no claim, make their own claim and enter the critical section. To avoid this

```
{ Solution 2 }
var claim1, claim2: Boolean;
begin
    claim1 := false; claim2 := false;

    cobegin

        P1:   repeat
                  claim1 := true;
                  repeat { do nothing } until not claim2;
                  critical_section_1;
                  claim1 := false;
                  non_critical_section_1
              until false;

        P2:   repeat
                  claim2 := true;
                  repeat { do nothing } until not claim1;
                  critical_section_2;
                  claim2 := false;
                  non_critical_section_2
              until false

    coend
end
```

Program 3.6

situation, suppose each process makes its claim before discovering whether the other has a claim pending. Our revised solution is shown as program 3.6.

As with the previous solution, the worst case occurs when the two processes proceed perfectly synchronised. This time, however, while we do ensure that the two processes are never in their critical sections together, we can have the situation where each may be

```
{ Solution 3}
var claim1, claim2: Boolean;
begin
    claim1 := false; claim2 := false;

    cobegin

        P1:   repeat
                  claim1 := true;
                  if claim2 then
                  begin
                      claim1 := false;
                      repeat { do nothing } until not claim2;
                      claim1 := true
                  end;
                  critical__section__1;
                  claim1 := false;
                  non__critical__section__1
              until false;

        P2:   repeat
                  claim2 := true;
                  if claim1 then
                  begin
                      claim2 := false;
                      repeat { do nothing } until not claim1;
                      claim2 := true
                  end;
                  critical__section__2;
                  claim2 := false;
                  non__critical__section__2
              until false

    coend
end
```

Program 3.7

waiting for the other to release its claim, neither will, and thus no progress can be made at all.

This solution is unsatisfactory because each process makes a claim, and then waits for the other to release its claim, which will not happen because neither will complete its critical section. Suppose then that we say that if, having made a claim, a process finds that the other one has also made a claim, it withdraws its own claim until the other process has completed its critical section and released its claim. Our third solution now appears as program 3.7.

Although we have increased the complexity, careful examination will show that this solution can suffer from exactly the same difficulty as solution 1 (program 3.5), namely that if the two processes proceed in total synchronism, they can arrive in their respective critical sections simultaneously. Let us therefore attempt to solve the problem using a totally different approach. Instead of each process having its own *claim* variable, we will introduce an independent variable called *turn* which indicates which process may enter its critical section. Thus program 3.8 illustrates our fourth solution.

```
{ Solution 4 }
type process__id = 1..2;  { in this example }
var turn: process__id;
begin
    turn := 1;    { arbitrarily }

    cobegin

    P1:   repeat
              repeat { do nothing } until turn = 1;
              critical__section__1;
              turn := 2;
              non__critical__section__1
          until false

    P2:   repeat
              repeat { do nothing } until turn = 2;
              critical__section__2;
              turn := 1;
              non__critical__section__2
          until false

    coend
end
```

Program 3.8

Program 3.8 will certainly ensure that the two critical sections are not entered simultaneously, and neither will either of them be delayed indefinitely waiting for the other to change the value of *turn*, but here we are violating ground rule number 3. This solution causes the two critical sections to be executed strictly alternately, and hence if $P1$ (say) was proceeding quickly enough to try to enter its critical section more frequently than $P2$, then $P1$ would be slowed down to the speed of *P2*. Worse still, if *P2* were to fail to leave its non-critical section, *P1* would be unable to proceed at all.

Solutions 1 and 3 (programs 3.5 and 3.7) are incorrect because they violate ground rule number 1. There is presumably therefore a danger that the two processes will interfere in such a way that the program will produce incorrect results. Solutions 2 and 4 (programs 3.6 and 3.8) on the other hand illustrate another kind of concurrency problem, in which processes are prevented from making progress, even though the computations they have executed so far are (presumably) correct.

As we have already discussed, solution 2 can lead to the situation where both processes are each waiting for the other, and neither can proceed. We describe this situation as *deadlock*. If we now consider solution 4, deadlock will not arise, since the two processes will never be waiting simultaneously to enter their respective critical sections, but it could happen that process *P1* (say) is unable to enter its critical section because of the actions of process *P2* in its non-critical section. Thus, since process *P2* is (presumably) still continuing to do useful work, but at the same time is unwittingly (or perhaps even maliciously!) preventing *P1* from progressing, we say that *P1* is suffering from *starvation*. In the case where more than two processes are involved in a critical section situation (we shall meet this again in the exercises to this chapter in section 3.10), it is also possible for starvation to occur as a result of two (or more) processes conspiring to prevent another process from entering its critical section, even though the "conspirators" are proceeding quite happily.

3.4 Dekker's/Peterson's Solution

The first correct solution to the problem was invented by Dekker, and it uses a combination of the techniques of claims and an independent arbiter. Each process makes a claim, and then inspects the claim variable of the other process. If there is no claim from the other process, then the critical section may be entered, but if the other process is making a simultaneous claim, then an appeal is made to the arbitrating variable *turn*. The full solution is given as program 3.9.

Dekker's solution to the critical section problem was the first solution which satisfied all of the ground rules, and in fact Dijkstra has proved this solution to be correct. A somewhat simpler formulation due

```
{ Dekker's solution }
type process__id = 1..2;
var claim1, claim2: Boolean; turn: process__id;
begin
    claim1 := false; claim2 := false; turn := 1;

    cobegin

        P1:  repeat
                claim1 := true;
                while claim2 do
                begin
                    claim1 := false;
                    repeat { do nothing } until turn = 1;
                    claim1 := true
                end;
                critical__section__1;
                claim1 := false; turn := 2;
                non__critical__section__1
             until false;

        P2:  repeat
                claim2 := true;
                while claim1 do
                begin
                    claim2 := false;
                    repeat { do nothing } until turn = 2;
                    claim2 := true
                end;
                critical__section__2;
                claim2 := false; turn := 1;
                non__critical__section__2
             until false

    coend
end
```

Program 3.9

to Peterson is presented as program 3.10. It is interesting, however, to observe that this pair of concurrent processes requires only the memory interlock to allow the method to work, and that a minor increase in hardware assistance will give rise to a considerable reduction in complexity.

```
{ Peterson's solution }
type process__id = 1..2;
var claim1, claim2: Boolean; turn: process__id;
begin
    claim1 := false; claim2 := false;

    cobegin

        P1:    repeat
                   claim1 := true;
                   turn := 2;
                   repeat { do nothing } until
                            not claim2 or turn = 1;
                   critical__section__1;
                   claim1 := false;
                   non__critical__section__1
               until false;

        P2:    repeat
                   claim2 := true;
                   turn := 1;
                   repeat { do nothing } until
                            not claim1 or turn = 2;
                   critical__section__2;
                   claim2 := false;
                   non__critical__section__2
               until false

    coend
end
```

Program 3.10

3.5   A Hardware-Assisted Solution

Many present-day computers provide a machine instruction which implements a *test and set* function, i.e. the ability to test the value of a memory location, and then to alter that value within the same instruction. Any computer which permits the programmer to alter the value of a memory word (or byte) and generate a condition code based on the *old* value of the memory location is capable of providing such a feature. The only constraint is that the operation must be indivisible. The PDP11 *swap byte* instruction, for instance, provides this facility, as does the TAS instruction of the M68000 family of processors. The essential action of such an instruction may be described by a Pascal function:

```
(atomic) function TestAndSet (var b: Boolean): Boolean;
begin
    TestAndSet := b;
    b := true
end
```

The word *atomic* is intended to remind us that this operation must be indivisible and that no interference with the variable *b* is permitted during the execution of this function. A much more elegant solution to the critical section problem can now be given as shown in program 3.11 making use of the *TestAndSet* function.

Each process in this method uses *TestAndSet* to set the value of *exclude* to *true*. If *exclude* was already *true*, then the function would return a *true* value and the process would have to wait. If the previous value of *exclude* was false however, the function will set it to true but return a false result, thus allowing the process to enter its critical section. The setting of *exclude* to *true* within the same operation ensures that no other process can see a *false* value of *exclude* while the first process is manipulating the variable.

3.6   Mutual Exclusion using Semaphores

In each of the previous examples, we see that each process contains the statement:

repeat { do nothing } **until** ... ;

or equivalently (as in program 3.11):

while ... **do** { nothing };

which is an effective way of wasting time whilst waiting for some condition to become true. Processes employing this technique are simply making the same test over and over again until it is found to be true (or false). In the world of sequential programming this would be a very strange construct indeed, resulting as it does in an infinite loop, since the body of the loop does nothing and therefore can have no effect on the outcome of the test. In the world of concurrent programming however, the statement is merely a method of waiting until some external influence (i.e. the action of another concurrent process) is

```
var exclude: Boolean;
begin
     exclude := false;

   cobegin

       P1:   repeat
                while TestAndSet (exclude) do { nothing };
                critical__section__1;
                exclude := false;
                non__critical__section__1
             until false;

       P2:   repeat
                while TestAndSet (exclude) do { nothing };
                critical__section__2;
                exclude := false;
                non__critical__section__2
             until false

   coend
end
```

Program 3.11

brought to bear which will change the result of the test. This is the so-called *busy waiting* condition. Perhaps a more sensible approach would be to allow the process to indicate that it can proceed no further until a particular condition is satisfied, and simply "go to sleep". It will then be the responsibility of another process not only to satisfy the condition, but also to "wake up" any process which is waiting for the condition to be satisfied. This may be achieved by introducing the semaphore (due to Dijkstra) and a pair of operations to manipulate semaphores. In his original paper, Dijkstra called these operations *P* and *V*, but more meaningful names (at least to native English speakers) *wait* and *signal* will be used in this book.

In its simplest form, a *semaphore* may be thought of as a Boolean variable, corresponding to a condition which must be satisfied before a process can proceed, but as we shall see there must also be some additional underlying mechanism. Such a semaphore is called a *binary* semaphore. Later on, we shall examine an extended form of semaphore whose values are not restricted to just true or false. For the present, though, a suitable type definition for a binary semaphore might be:

type *semaphore* = *Boolean*;

We have to assume that the two operations, which by the way are the only operations permitted on semaphores, are atomic. Making this assumption, we define the two operations in terms of the following procedures:

```
(atomic) procedure wait (var s: semaphore);
begin
    if not s then
        "put calling process to sleep"
    else s := false
end
```

and:

```
(atomic) procedure signal (var s: semaphore);
begin
    if "there is a sleeping process" then
        "wake up a sleeping process"
    else s := true
end
```

Program 3.12 shows a solution to the critical section problem making use of a binary semaphore and the operations *wait* and *signal*.

In our consideration of the various solutions to the critical section problem, we have examined the problem only with a view to avoiding interference between processes. The necessity for a critical section implies that access is required to a shared resource, and that interference from another process must be avoided while any process is making use of the shared resource. Thus, for example, in the solution presented in program 3.12, which solves the critical section problem by using a semaphore, the semaphore is used only so that one process may inform the other(s) of the fact that it is about to enter, or has just left, its critical section. In other words, the semaphore is used to exchange timing information between the processes to enforce mutual exclusion from critical sections.

```
var mutex: semaphore;
begin
    mutex := true;

    cobegin
        P1:  repeat
                wait (mutex);
                critical_section_1;
                signal (mutex);
                non_critical_section_1
             until false;

        P2:  repeat
                wait (mutex);
                critical_section_2;
                signal (mutex);
                non_critical_section_2
             until false

    coend
end
```
                Program 3.12

3.7   Semaphores as Timing Signals

Semaphores may be used in a rather more general way than merely to enforce mutual exclusion. There may be other conditions which processes must wait for and which must be signalled between processes. We give now an example showing how semaphores may be used purely as timing signals, and also showing that semaphores do not have to be used in the symmetric way that we have seen in the critical section example. It also shows the use of semaphores among a set of more than two processes.

We assume that there are a set of *n* processes whose function is to carry out a particular task at regular intervals (a different interval for each task). Each of these processes must therefore be triggered at a certain point in time. To co-ordinate the restarting of each process, a *scheduler* process is introduced, and a *timer* process is also used to provide the basic clock pulses to drive the whole system. The timer is an independent process which ticks away at its own rate, and after a fixed number of its own ticks signals a semaphore. The scheduler waits on this semaphore, and when it is awoken by the timer it makes decisions about which processes, if any, must be triggered to perform their tasks. The variables in use in this program are:

int	array of values indicating the intervals at which the various tasks need to be awoken.
deadline	array local to the scheduler indicating the time at which each of the task processes must be awoken.
start	array of semaphores by which the scheduler communicates with the task processes.
tim	semaphore for timer process to communicate with the scheduler.

The full text of the program is given as program 3.13, and we shall discuss the component processes in order of increasing interest.

The processes represented by the code labelled *taski* are the controlling tasks which have to be activated at regular intervals. We neither know nor care what is the task in detail which each has to carry out. Suffice it to observe that each one is an infinite loop, being awoken by the scheduler at the appropriate time, performing its individual task, and then becoming inactive until the next deadline is reached.

The *timer* process represents a free running clock which decrements a local variable t from some initial value, and generates a signal when its value reaches zero. The value of t is then re-initialised to its former value, and the cycle is repeated. This might be thought of as representing the hardware clock of a computer system which generates a signal (i.e. an interrupt) at regular intervals. Some computers offer the facilities of a programmable *interval timer*, where the initial value of the clock's local variable can be set by program.

The *scheduler* process begins by waiting for the timer to activate it, which happens at regular intervals. These intervals must of course be considerably shorter than the intervals at which the processes must be awakened, so that the deadlines for the tasks are not missed. Whenever the scheduler is awoken, it decreases the *deadline* value for each task, indicating that the deadline has moved one

```
const      n = ... ; { number of tasks }
var   int, deadline:  array [1..n] of integer;
      start: array [1..n] of semaphore;
      tim:   semaphore;
      t:     integer; tsk:    1..n;   { local variables }
begin
      tim := false; initialise (int, deadline, start);
            { the initial values of int are defined by the problem,
                deadline is initialised to be the same as int, and
                each element of the array start is set to false }

   cobegin

      timer:        repeat
                       t := "number of timer pulses
                           between scheduler pulses";
                       repeat t := t - 1 until t < = 0;
                       signal (tim)
                    until false;

      scheduler: repeat
                       wait (tim);
                       for tsk := 1 to n do
                       begin
                          deadline[tsk] :=
                                deadline[tsk] - 1;
                          if deadline[tsk] < = 0 then
                          begin
                             deadline[tsk] := int[tsk];
                             signal (start[tsk])
                          end
                       end
                    until false;

      ...
      { n tasks of which the i-th is represented as follows: }
      taski:        repeat
                       wait (start[i]);
                       perform_task_i
                    until false;

      ...
   coend
end
```

Program 3.13

scheduler time interval closer. If by so doing, the deadline for any task is reached (or possibly passed), the corresponding semaphore is signalled, thus causing the task to be re-activated. At the same time, the scheduler recomputes the deadline for that task using the interval for that particular process.

In this example, the semaphore mechanisms are being used purely for the purposes of passing timing information between concurrent activities, so that the scheduler can receive basic timing information from the timer, and disseminate it as appropriate amongst the tasks being scheduled.

3.8   Semaphores for Exchanging Information

Let us now consider two concurrent processes, one of which is responsible for generating messages and passing them on to the other process which makes use of them as shown in Figure 3.1. The first process may be described as a *producer* of messages while the second may be called a *consumer*. Many examples can be found of processes which are required to send messages to each other, most frequently in operating systems. One such example might be of a process which has the responsibility of "driving" an output device such as a printer, and to which another process passes lines of generated text. The text generator process could then be called the producer, and the printer driving process would be the consumer, the messages in this case being the lines of text.

If we assume for the moment that these two processes continue to produce and consume indefinitely, clearly they must communicate with one another, and so we may describe the action of the producer by:

> **repeat**
>   "produce message";
>   "wait until message is consumed"
> **until** *false*

and the consumer process may be described similarly:

> **repeat**
>   "wait until message is produced";
>   "consume message"
> **until** *false*

The method by which the producer and consumer processes communicate with one another may also be through the use of

Figure 3.1.

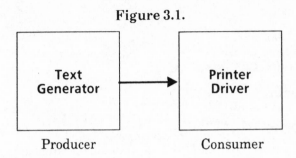

semaphores. A semaphore may be used for the producer to signal to the consumer that a message has been produced, and the consumer may use another semaphore to signal to the producer that the last message has been consumed, and that the consumer is now ready to receive another one. The programmed version of this solution is given as program 3.14.

In this example, the events which are being waited for and signalled are not merely "permission" to enter a critical section, but are conditions which have a direct bearing upon the subsequent behaviour of each process. This demonstrates that the semaphore is a much more powerful construct in concurrent programming than simply a signalling mechanism for mutual exclusion from critical sections.

While the producer/consumer example given above serves well to illustrate another use of the semaphore, it is imprecise in its specification of what actually happens to the message as it passes from producer to consumer, and this particular example has another disadvantage as well. It uses only a single message, implying that each message produced must be consumed before another can be produced. Thus the two processes must advance perfectly synchronised, and if the consumer should be delayed in disposing of a message, then the producer would be delayed too. Similarly, if the producer is delayed in generating any message, then the consumer is correspondingly delayed. A standard technique for smoothing out local variations in the speed of operation of processes is to use a *buffer*. In this case, we may insert a buffer between the producer and consumer processes as shown in figure 3.2, so that even if the consumer is delayed in attempting to consume a message, the producer may continue to produce messages and place them in the buffer. If the producer is

```
var p, c: semaphore;
begin
    p := false; c := false;

    cobegin

    Producer:  repeat
                  produce__message;
                  signal (p);      { message produced }
                  wait (c)
               until false;

    Consumer: repeat
                  wait (p);
                  consume__message;
                  signal (c)       { message consumed }
               until false

    coend
end
```

Program 3.14

subsequently delayed, the consumer is able to occupy its time usefully in "clearing the backlog" of messages waiting in the buffer. Of course, if there truly are no messages for the consumer (i.e. the buffer is empty) then the consumer must wait because there will be nothing for it to do. It is also the case that no practical implementation of a message buffer could afford to allow the producer to generate an indefinite number of messages without the consumer taking some out, that is we could expect only a finite number of messages to be buffered. This problem is known as the *bounded buffer problem*. Clearly it is necessary to prevent the producer from generating messages when the

Figure 3.2.

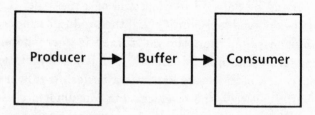

buffer is "full". However, despite the necessity for both producer and consumer to be delayed occasionally, we would certainly expect a buffered message system to smooth out local variations in the speeds of both processes, so that overall the performance (i.e. the time to pass some arbitrary number of messages) would be better than with the unbuffered system. Using these notions of a buffered message passing scheme, program 3.15 describes the actions of the producer and consumer processes .

cobegin

Producer: **repeat**
      "produce message";
      if "buffer is full" **then**
          "wait until buffer not full";
      "place message in buffer"
   until *false*;

Consumer: **repeat**
      if "buffer is empty" **then**
          "wait until buffer not empty";
      "retrieve message from buffer";
      "consume message"
   until *false*

coend

Program 3.15

In the same way as we used semaphores in the unbuffered message case, so we can use semaphores to indicate changes in the "fullness" or "emptiness" of the buffer. The producer will have to wait if a semaphore indicates that the buffer is completely full, and the only way that the buffer will cease to be full is by the consumer taking a message out. Thus the consumer can be responsible for signalling to the waiting producer process. In a precisely symmetric way, the consumer must wait if a semaphore indicates that the whole buffer is empty, and the producer can signal if it puts a message into the buffer.

By introducing the idea of a buffer, to which both the producer and consumer have access, we have added an additional complication to the problem, in that the use of a shared resource has now become explicit. In program 3.14, the mechanism by which a message passed from producer to consumer was not defined precisely, and the implicit assumption was made that the underlying mechanism would carry out this task correctly. In program 3.16, which shows a solution including all the implementation details, the accesses to the buffer have now become explicit, which implies that the mutual exclusion required to prevent undesirable interference must also be made explicit.

```
const BufferCapacity = ... ;
var  not_full, not_empty, mutex: semaphore;
     n:   0..BufferCapacity;
begin
     mutex := true; not_full := true;
     not_empty := false; n := 0;

     cobegin

     Producer:  repeat
                    produce_message;
                    if n = BufferCapacity then
                                   wait (not_full);
                    wait (mutex);
                    place_message_in_buffer;
                    n := n + 1;
                    if n = 1 then signal (not_empty);
                    signal (mutex)
                until false;

     Consumer:  repeat
                    if n = 0 then wait (not_empty);
                    wait (mutex);
                    retrieve_message_from_buffer;
                    n := n - 1;
                    if n = BufferCapacity-1 then
                                   signal (not_full);
                    signal (mutex)
                until false

     coend
end
```

Program 3.16

Notice how in this program we have found it necessary to introduce a special variable n to keep track of the number of messages in the buffer. This variable must be tested before a *wait* is executed in order to find out whether there is a message for the consumer to retrieve or a position in which the producer may place a message. There is a sense in which the test part of the *wait* operation appears to be duplicating the test that has already been made. However, the test for the number of messages in the buffer and the *wait* operation can not be made indivisible, and therefore there could be interleavings which might cause the program to behave incorrectly.

3.9   Non-Binary Semaphores

This observation identifies a serious flaw in the program. Clearly the two *wait* operations at the beginning of each process must be executed in the order shown. This is because, if the *mutex* semaphore was claimed (by the *wait* operation) and then the process subsequently found that it was unable to proceed because the condition on which the next *wait* was operating was false, no other process would be able to change the condition because it would be unable to obtain control of the *mutex* semaphore. But the test that has to be performed to discover whether the first *wait* is necessary requires inspection of the variable n which is itself shared, and therefore should be protected by a critical section. Also, it is perfectly possible for either process to be interrupted between the testing of the value of n and the subsequent *wait* operation, which may lead to incorrect behaviour of the program.

This difficulty can be overcome by calling the *wait(mutex)* first in each process, and introducing an additional test into the program to determine whether the condition is satisfied, and if not, performing a *signal(mutex)* to release the critical section, as shown in program 3.17. A more elegant solution can be obtained however, by extending the definition of a semaphore as was hinted at earlier, and redefining the *wait* and *signal* operations. Instead of a semaphore taking only the values *true* and *false* (i.e. a binary semaphore) we will allow the semaphore to take an *integer* value. A type definition for the extended semaphore might be:

type *semaphore* $=$ *integer*;

and then the amended definitions of *wait* and *signal* would be:

```
const BufferCapacity = ... ;
var   not__full, not__empty, mutex:  semaphore;
      n:     0..BufferCapacity;
begin
    mutex := true; not__full := false;
    not__empty := false; n := 0;

    cobegin

        Producer:    repeat
                        produce__message;
                        wait (mutex);
                        if n = BufferCapacity then
                        begin
                           signal (mutex);
                           wait (not__full);
                           wait (mutex)
                        end;
                        place__message__in__buffer;
                        n := n + 1;
                        if n = 1 then signal (not__empty);
                        signal (mutex)
                     until false;

        Consumer:    repeat
                        if n = BufferCapacity then
                        begin
                           signal (mutex);
                           wait (not__empty);
                           wait (mutex)
                        end;
                        retrieve__message__from__buffer;
                        n := n - 1;
                        if n = BufferCapacity-1 then
                                    signal (not__full);
                        signal (mutex)
                     until false

    coend
end
```

Program 3.17

```
(atomic) procedure wait (var s: semaphore);
begin
  s := s - 1;
  if s < 0 then "put calling process to sleep"
end
```

and:

```
(atomic) procedure signal (var s: semaphore);
begin
  s := s + 1;
  if s < = 0 then "wake up a sleeping process"
end
```

With these definitions, we are able to observe a number of interesting properties of the semaphore. Firstly, as we shall see shortly when we return to the bounded message buffer problem, the initial value of the semaphore represents the number of resources that we are trying to protect with this semaphore, and as the processes execute *wait* operations on it the value of the semaphore decreases, so that at any time the numerical value of the semaphore equals the number of resources which are still available to be allocated so long as the value is positive. Of course, in the critical section problem, where we require mutual exclusion from the sensitive sections of code, the initial value of the semaphore must be 1. The absolute value of a semaphore when its value is negative is also of significance. Since the semaphore is decreased by 1 for every *wait* operation, and each time that value is less than zero a process is put to sleep, the absolute value of a negative semaphore is equal to the number of processes currently waiting for *signal*s on that semaphore. If we were to think of processes waiting on a semaphore as forming a queue, then the absolute value of the semaphore is equal to the length of the queue. The **if** clause within the procedure *signal* makes use of this fact by testing to see if it has just incremented the semaphore from a negative value. If so, it is known that there must be at least one process waiting, and a process is therefore awoken.

Using this extended version of the semaphore mechanism, we may rewrite our solution to the message buffer problem, making use of

```
const BufferCapacity = ... ;
var mutex, full, empty: semaphore;
begin
    mutex := 1; full := 0; empty := BufferCapacity;

    cobegin

        Producer:   repeat
                        produce__message;
                        wait (empty); { wait for an empty slot }
                        wait (mutex);
                        place__message__in__buffer;
                        signal (full);
                        signal (mutex)
                    until false;

        Consumer:   repeat
                        wait (full);
                            { wait for at least one message }
                        wait (mutex);
                        retrieve__message__from__buffer;
                        signal (empty);
                        signal (mutex);
                        consume__message
                    until false

    coend
end
```

Program 3.18

the integer-valued semaphore to keep a count of the number of messages in the buffer, while another indicates how many empty places are still left in the buffer. Program 3.18 gives an alternative concurrent program making use of these additional facilities.

We have seen several examples of concurrent programs in this chapter, including a number of different ways in which communication and co-operation between independent processes running in parallel can be achieved. However, the use of semaphores is only one method of achieving this end. In the following chapter, we shall examine some ways of providing more structured constructs for inter-process communication.

3.10 Exercises

3.1 In the example of access to a shared disk (example 2 on page 45), two possible interleavings of the instructions of processes *P1* and *P2* were given. Enumerate *all* the possible interleavings of the two sequences of instructions (there should be six of them), indicating which of them lead to correct and which to incorrect results.

3.2 Repeat exercise 3.1 for the example in which a shared variable is incremented. (Note that there are now twenty possible interleavings.)

3.3 Satisfy yourself that program 3.7 is an incorrect solution to the critical section problem by constructing an interleaving of the statements which causes both *P1* and *P2* to enter their critical sections simultaneously.

3.4 Give informal arguments to show that Dekker's and Peterson's methods cannot give rise to starvation.

3.5 Program 3.19 shows Dijkstra's solution to the n-process critical section problem (for $n > 2$) where each process consists of a call to the procedure *process* with its own identity i as the parameter. Describe the purpose of the global arrays b and c and the global variable *turn*, and describe also how the method satisfies the ground rules of the critical section problem. Give an explanation also of the purpose of the "fictitious" process zero.

3.6 Show that starvation could occur in the solution given in program 3.19.

```
{ Dijkstra's generalisation of Dekker's method }
type process__id : 0..n;
var b, c : array [process__id] of Boolean; turn : process__id;

procedure process (i : process__id);
var j : process__id; ok : Boolean;
begin
    repeat
        b[i] := false;
        repeat
            while turn <> i do
            begin
                c[i] := true;
                if b[turn] then turn := i
            end;
            c[i] := false;
            ok := true;
            for j := 1 to n do
            if j <> i then ok := ok and c[j]
        until ok;
        critical__section (i);
        c[i] := true; b[i] := true;
        turn := 0;
        non__critical__section (i)
    until false
end; { process }

begin { main program }
    for turn := 0 to n do
    begin
        b[turn] := true; c[turn] := true
    end;
    turn := 0;
    cobegin
        process (1);
        process (2);
        ...
        process (i);
        ...
    coend
end
```

Program 3.19

3.7 [Bakery Algorithm - Lamport] Program 3.20 gives an alternative version of the program to solve the n-process critical section problem. Show that this program also satisfies the ground rules, and explain why this solution will not suffer from starvation.

3.8 Some computers have a swap-byte (*SWAB*) instruction which has the effect of reversing the values of two bytes in memory. (In practice, this usually takes the form of exchanging the two bytes within a single 16-bit word.) Write a Pascal procedure (or function) in the style of the Pascal version of *TestAndSet*, as in section 3.5, to describe the action of *SWAB*, and show how it could be used to solve the critical section problem.

3.9 Show that the *TestAndSet* method could give rise to starvation, and explain why this is unlikely to happen in practice.

3.10 The Sleeping Barber (Dijkstra):
A barber's shop with a separate waiting room is so arranged that the door by which the customers enter the waiting room is only open when the door into the room containing the barber's chair is closed and vice versa. After visiting the barber, customers leave the shop by another exit.
When the barber first arrives for work, or when he has finished serving a customer, he opens the door from the cutting room into the waiting room to see if there are any customers waiting. If there are, he invites the first of them into the cutting room, closes the door and begins to cut the customer's hair. If the waiting room is empty, he closes the door and goes to sleep in his chair.
When a customer arrives, if he finds the waiting room empty, he opens the door into the barber's room. If he finds the barber asleep, he wakes him up and begins to have his hair cut. If the barber is busy, or if he finds other customers in the waiting room, he simply sits down and waits his turn to be served.
By considering the barber and each of his customers as a separate process, outline a program which describes the

```
{ Lamport's Bakery algorithm }
type process_id : 1..n;
var   choosing : array [process_id] of Boolean;
      number : array [process_id] of integer;
      i : process_id;

{ function max returns the maximum value in
  elements 1..n of the array number }

procedure process (i : process_id);
var j : process_id;
begin
  repeat
    choosing [i] := true;
    number [i] := 1 + max (number, 1, n);
    choosing [i] := false;
    for j := 1 to n do
    begin
      repeat until not choosing [j];
      repeat until not (number [j] = 0)
                or (number [j] > number [i])
                or ((number [j] = number [i]) and (j > = i))
    end;
    critical_section (i);
    number [i] := 0;
    non_critical_section (i)
  until false
end; { process }

begin { main program }
  for i := 1 to n do
  begin
    number [i] := 0;
    choosing [i] := false
  end;

  cobegin
    process (1);
    process (2);
    ...
    process (i);
    ...
  coend
end
```

Program 3.20

behaviour of this situation, using semaphores to describe the communication between the processes.

3.11   The Dining Philosophers (Dijkstra):
Five philosophers are seated round a circular table. Each philosopher has in front of him a plate (initially empty) and in the centre of the table is a large bowl of spaghetti. Between each pair of adjacent philosophers is a fork. The philosophers spend their time alternating between thinking and eating. When they are thinking, they do so without interacting with the other philosophers. In order to eat, however, a philosopher must obtain the two forks on either side of his plate in order to be able to help himself to spaghetti from the bowl. When a philosopher is eating, therefore, neither of his neighbours can be eating at the same time.

Design a concurrent program in which the five philosophers are represented by processes, and where the interaction between the philosophers (i.e. the acquisition and relinquishment of forks) is controlled by the use of semaphores.

3.12   Old fairground machines can still occasionally be found which stamp out one's name or other message on an aluminium strip. The customer (after paying his money, of course) would move a pointer to point to a particular letter and press a lever to cause that letter to be impressed upon the strip. The pointer would then be moved to another letter and the lever pressed again.

You are required to design an electronic version of such a device, in which there are 26 processes whose sole purpose is to impress a particular letter on the strip, and a similar process for causing a space to appear. Another process is merely waiting for the button (the re-engineered lever) to be pressed, and finally there is a process which, on being informed that the button has been pressed, discovers the current position of the pointer (which could be any one of the 26 letters of the alphabet or a space), and instructs the appropriate "stamping" process to perform its work. Use semaphores to show how a concurrent program might be designed to act in the manner described.

3.13   Programming exercise: Try to illustrate the phenomenon of interference using the following example.

A bank holds its customers' accounts on a central computer to which the branches of the bank may have interactive access. It is clear that interference may take place if simultaneous accesses to the same account record occur (presumably from different branches). This situation can be modelled by the following simple simulation.

Let there be m customers (i.e. accounts), and assume that only three types of transaction are permitted - *credit*, *debit* and *internal transfer*. For the *debit* and *credit* transactions, an account number and an amount are supplied, and the effect of the transaction is to decrease or increase the balance of the specified account by the specified amount. The *transfer* transaction takes a source and destination account number and an amount, decrementing the source balance and incrementing the destination balance by the amount specified.

In order to simulate substantial processing for each transaction, your program should read the balance of an account into a local variable, update the local variable as appropriate, and write back the new value to the balance.

Choose a number n, and write a program which creates three concurrent processes for processing a sequence of n credits, n debits and n transfers respectively. The account numbers involved in each transaction should be chosen at random. If the accounts all begin with a known balance, and if every transaction specifies the same amount, then the total of all the balances at the end of the program should be the same as the total of all the balances at the start of the program. If this is not the case, then (assuming the program is correct) we must assume that interference has taken place.

Clearly the probability of interference occurring may be increased by increasing n and/or decreasing m. A delay could be introduced during the processing of a transaction, i.e. after reading the account balance into the local variable, and before writing back the new value, and this would also increase the probability of interference occurring.

Once interference has been demonstrated, modify your program to include the code to implement the Dekker/Peterson solution, and observe that the interference no longer occurs (or does it?).
Also use your version of *TestAndSet* to prevent the interference.

How restrictive are the solutions you have provided? Do they enforce an unnecessary degree of sequentiality? If so, how would you change your strategy to make them less restrictive?

The banking model could be made more realistic by creating a separate process for each transaction, rather than creating a process for a sequence of transactions of each type. This would clearly have the effect of increasing the probability of interference occurring, but your earlier solutions should still prevent this happening.
The introduction of parallel *transfer* transactions could give rise to another kind of concurrency problem. Can you say what this is, how it might occur, and what measures could be taken to prevent it?

4
High-Level Concurrency
Constructs - Shared Data

In the previous chapter we considered the basic problem of communication between processes, and reduced it to the problem of preventing two processes from accessing the same shared resources simultaneously. It should be clear that from such mechanisms it is possible to construct a large number of different methods for communication. It is also clear that the relationship between the low-level mechanisms described in the previous chapter and the higher-level constructs is similar to the relationship between a low-level assembly language program and the corresponding program in a high-level language; the first provides a basic mechanism, which clearly is sufficient, if inconvenient, to implement all the necessary synchronisation. The second expresses the solution to the problem in a much more "problem oriented" fashion.

In this chapter we shall consider a number of high-level constructs which have been proposed which allow a more structured approach to many inter-process communication/synchronisation problems. In the same way that the use of high-level languages allows the programmer to express his algorithms in a more natural way, and hence will make the inclusion of simple logical errors less likely, so the use of high-level synchronisation constructs in concurrent programs will also tend to reduce the incidence of elementary concurrent programming errors.

To take a small example, consider program 4.1, which uses binary semaphores to provide an implementation of the critical section problem (c.f. program 3.12).

This program contains what might be considered as an elementary programming error in *P2* (indicated by { !!!!!! }) in which the *wait* statement has been erroneously inserted instead of a *signal*

```
        var mutex: semaphore;
        begin
            mutex := true;

            cobegin

                P1:   repeat
                          wait (mutex);
                          critical__section__1;
                          signal (mutex);
                          non__critical__section__1
                      until false;

                P2:   repeat
                          wait (mutex);
                          critical__section__2;
                          wait (mutex);                    { !!!!!! }
                          non__critical__section__2
                      until false

            coend

        end
```

Program 4.1

statement, a mistake as easy to make as (say) decrementing a variable when it should be incremented. Another example is shown as program 4.2.

In this case, the programmer has erroneously interchanged the *signal* and *wait* statements in process *P1* (again indicated by the "comments" { !!!!!! }). It is clear that in the first example, the error is going to have the effect of preventing all progress. This is because the first time *P2* obtains access to its critical section, by correctly using the semaphore *mutex*, it will complete the critical section and then become blocked at the erroneous *wait* statement. Process *P1* meanwhile may or may not have made some prior accesses to its critical section, but now that process *P2* has blocked itself, *P1* will also become blocked as a result of its own (correct) *wait* statement.

In some sense the second example represents an even more disastrous error. In this case, the *signal* and *wait* statements have been interchanged and there is no longer any protection on the critical section in process *P1*. In fact, the process as written has almost reversed the roles of the critical and non-critical sections in this

```
var mutex: semaphore;
begin
    mutex := true;

  cobegin

    P1:  repeat
            signal (mutex);              { !!!!!! }
            critical__section__1;
            wait (mutex);                { !!!!!! }
            non__critical__section__1
         until false;

    P2:  repeat
            wait (mutex);
            critical__section__2;
            signal (mutex);
            non__critical__section__2
         until false

  coend

end
```

Program 4.2

process except that the presence of the statement *signal (mutex)* at the beginning of *P1* has effectively caused a slight change in the initial value of *mutex*. As a result neither process will be delayed at a *wait* statement, and mutual exclusion will never occur.

There is another sense in which a mutual exclusion semaphore lacks robustness against programming errors, and this problem has a parallel with the notion of scope of variables in a high-level sequential programming language. In the examples given above, correction of the errors will give a program which correctly provides mutual exclusion of the critical sections, but cannot guarantee that the shared resources which the semaphore operations are designed to protect are only accessed within the critical sections controlled by these semaphore operations. That is, we cannot be sure that the shared resources are not accessed outside the critical sections. We now consider some possible structures which attempt to overcome these difficulties.

A third form of error which could also arise as a result of the misuse of semaphores is concerned with incorrect initialisation of the mutual exclusion semaphore. Clearly, if *mutex* were to be initialised with the value *false* (instead of *true*) in program 3.12, then both *P1* and *P2* would be delayed indefinitely waiting for access to their respective critical sections.

4.1   Critical Regions

Brinch Hansen presents a program structure, originally proposed by Hoare, which both guarantees a correct use of critical sections, and provides a method of ensuring that shared variables are only accessed within appropriate critical sections. This construct is called a *critical region*. Brinch Hansen suggests that it should be possible to declare variables to have the attribute **shared**, and he proposes that an additional control structure called **region** should be provided. The **region** statement is used in a similar way to that in which the Pascal **with** statement is used, but the subject of the **region** statement is required to have the attribute **shared**. The semantics of the **region** statement then require that exclusive control of (i.e. access to) this shared variable is necessary before the body of the **region** is executed. Program 4.3 shows the solution of the canonical critical section problem using this construct.

```
type T = ...;

var v: shared T;

begin
    initialise (v);

    cobegin

        P1:   repeat
                  region v do critical__section__1;
                  non__critical__section__1
              until false;

        P2:   repeat
                  region v do critical__section__2;
                  non__critical__section__2
              until false

    coend

end
```
                   Program 4.3

It is clear that any compiler handling constructs of this type would be able to relieve the programmer of two onerous tasks; (i) to provide *wait* and *signal* operations on an appropriate semaphore to control access to the critical sections, and (ii) to ensure that the shared resource (the shared variable v in this case) is only accessed within the respective critical sections.

4.2   Conditional Critical Regions

We observed, during our discussion of the critical section problem in the previous chapter, and in particular during the examination of the bounded buffer problem, that mutual exclusion on its own is frequently not enough. It was sometimes possible, having obtained access to a shared resource, that the required action was not possible because of some other condition of the resource, and there was nothing to be gained (and everything to be lost) by allowing that process to keep control over the resource. It is therefore desirable to provide a mechanism whereby the process, having gained access to the resource only to find that it cannot proceed with its task, can release the resource so that another process is able to enter its critical section, change the state and thus satisfy the condition required by the first process.

It was recognised that the critical region construct on its own would provide no more than mutual exclusion, and that some extension of the mechanism would be necessary to provide the additional facilities required. The extension proposed by Brinch Hansen is called a *conditional critical region*, and contains a statement known as an **await** statement.

The **await** statement takes a Boolean expression as its argument, which, if it evaluates to a true value, will allow the process to execute, but if it evaluates to false, the process is forced to wait, giving up control of the critical region. This then allows another process to enter its critical region which will (hopefully) change the condition which is preventing the first process from continuing.

The general form of the conditional critical region is given as program 4.4, and we can see in this example that processing can in general take place both before and after the **await** statement. However, a more common occurrence is for the **await** statement to be found at the end, or, even more likely, at the beginning of the critical

Px: **begin**

.

region *v* **do**
begin

.

.

.

await *B(v)*;

.

.

.

end;

.

.

.

end

Program 4.4

region. The reason for this is not hard to find, and relates to the fact that if a critical section wishes to act upon some shared data, it is likely to check to see whether the data is in a suitable state (i.e. some predicate applied to the data is true) before it begins to operate on the data.

The question of when the **await** statement is used raises an important issue in the use of conditional critical regions, and indeed, in consideration of critical sections in general. We have assumed that the shared data structure which is to be protected must have some property which is always true; a consistency condition. This consistency condition is sometimes known as an *invariant*. The critical section is necessary because at some point during the manipulation of the data structure, the invariant is not true. We make the assumption that critical sections are well-behaved in the sense that the data structure, while it may be temporarily inconsistent during the execution of the critical section, always satisfies its invariant outside the critical section. Thus the critical section will always return the data structure to a consistent state on exit.

The **await** statement clearly has a similar responsiblity. The critical region is left on encountering an **await** statement with a false Boolean, and thus other processes may be allowed access to their critical regions and hence to the shared data. Such processes will clearly expect the invariant to be true of the data on entry to their critical regions, and hence processes using **await** must ensure that the invariant is also true immediately prior to executing the **await** statement.

4.3   Monitors

The critical region and its extended form, the conditional critical region, will provide most of the facilities which are required from a synchronisation and communication mechanism for co-operating concurrent processes, although it is not easy to see how the final example of Chapter 3, the scheduling of tasks, could be implemented using these constructs. Beyond the ability to check that shared data is not accessed outside a critical region, however, they do not apply any discipline to the way in which the shared data is manipulated. That is, once approval has been obtained for access to the shared data, there are no constraints on the operations which may be performed on that data. There is, therefore, an obligation on the programmer to ensure that the manipulations carried out on the data structure during the execution of the critical region do not leave the structure in an inconsistent state, i.e. the invariant is true on exit from the critical region.

To impose some controls over the way in which a shared data structure is manipulated, the next synchronisation construct we shall consider is an extension of the notion of *class* as found in the programming language Simula67. Simula67 is not a concurrent language, but some of the facilities it provides go some way to allowing the implementation of controlled communication between concurrent processes.

The Simula class allows the programmer to manipulate a data structure in a controlled way by making access to the data impossible except through a defined interface, consisting of a set of functions and/or procedures. Thus we can ensure that unconstrained interference with the data is impossible, since the creator of the class can define those, and only those, operations on the data which do not destroy the consistency of the data structure. Another feature of the class construct is that it encourages the use of abstract data types upon which operations can be defined without the client of these operations being burdened with the implementation details of the data type.

By compelling the user of the data structure to access it only through the defined operations, the author of a class can ensure that the concrete representation of the data (i.e. the local variables of the class) is in a consistent state on exit from the class. Furthermore, we can use the principle of the class to group together data and operations in a single structure. This property of the class is precisely what is required to maintain the integrity of a data structure when it is desired to operate upon it with a number of concurrent processes. The only difference between the Simula class and the shared data considered earlier is that Simula is a sequential language, and so does not need to worry about possible interference while the procedures and functions of a class are being executed.

Suppose then that a structure such as the Simula class were used to provide a *shared* abstract data object. The discussion above suggests that the consistency of the concrete data might be compromised if a process could access the data while another operation is in progress. The *monitor* construct, proposed by Hoare, provides the notion of a shared class, but goes on to insist that any process wishing to execute an operation of the class may do so only if no other process is currently accessing the data. If then we imagine our class as consisting of a set of (hidden) variables together with a set of (visible) procedures and functions, but with the additional restriction that only one process may be executing any of the procedures or functions at a time, then we have the synchronisation/communication mechanism known as a *monitor*.

In some ways the monitor is not unlike the critical region in that access to the components of the shared variable is only permitted using particular sections of the code. The principal difference is that the monitor provides a single object in which the data and the operations on that data are collected together in one place within the program. In other words, it is not necessary to broadcast all the details of the data structure to all the processes which might wish to use it, but merely provide operations (with appropriate parameters) which will manipulate the data structure on behalf of the processes. In this sense, it is the data structuring aspects - the so-called "information hiding" property - of the monitor which distinguishes it from the critical region.

Now as with the critical region, so with the monitor; there is a logical problem associated with giving exclusive rights of access to a data structure to a process which may be unable to use it for other reasons. It is then necessary for this process to relinquish control in order to let a second process have access to the data, while at the same time keeping some rights of access so that operations may be performed when the inhibiting condition is removed. The monitor therefore, like the conditional critical region, requires a mechanism for allowing a process which has control of the monitor, to relinquish it temporarily in order to allow another process to make modifications to the data structure and thus allow the first process to continue. Such a mechanism is provided in a monitor, and is called a *condition*.

In its operation, a condition is not dissimilar to a semaphore, and in fact a condition is manipulated using two primitives *signal* and *wait* which behave in a similar manner to the corresponding semaphore operations. A variable of type *condition* may only be declared within a monitor however, and therefore the operations can only be invoked by a process already in a monitor procedure or function. The effect of calling a *wait* operation on a condition is to cause the calling process to be suspended, and to relinquish, temporarily, control of the monitor. Another process may then enter the monitor, and it is to be hoped that eventually some other process will invoke the *signal* operation on the condition, at which time the waiting process can be resumed. A simple example will illustrate the notion of a monitor.

Suppose we have a resource for which a number of processes are competing, and the nature of the resource is such that only one process should be able to use the resource at any one time. It is therefore necessary for some constraints on the access to the resource to be enforced. We will assume that use of the resource will only be attempted after a successful request has been made to acquire it. Similarly, an indication must be given of the fact that access to the resource is no longer required. The monitor *SingleResource*, shown in program 4.5, will provide the controlled access necessary (provided all the competing processes obey the rules and use the resource only after a successful attempt to acquire it, and release it after use).

In looking at this simple monitor, we can make some observations about the data it is operating upon, and the way in which it does it. Firstly, we notice that the two variables which make up the data structure are accessible only within the monitor itself, i.e. *busy* and *NonBusy* are not visible to processes outside. Secondly, the only

```
SingleResource:
  monitor
    begin
      var  busy : Boolean;
           NonBusy : condition;

      procedure acquire;
        begin
          if busy then NonBusy .wait;
          busy := true
        end;     { acquire }

      procedure release;
        begin
          busy := false;
          NonBusy .signal
        end;     { release }

      { monitor initialisation }
      busy := false
    end;    { monitor SingleResource }
          Program 4.5
```

operations performed on the condition variable are the *wait* in *acquire*,
and the *signal* in *release*. In the monitor *SingleResource*, as in all other
instances, the condition variable is associated with some predicate of
the data structure which can be either *true* or *false*. In this simple case,
the condition *NonBusy* is directly associated with the falsity or truth of
the Boolean variable *busy*.

It is important to be aware of the sequence of events which
takes place when a *wait* or a *signal* is invoked, and the constraints on
where these operations may be used. When a *wait* is performed on a
condition, the effect is to send the calling process to sleep, thus
allowing another process to have access to the monitor. It is obvious
that this should not be allowed to happen when the data of the monitor
is in an inconsistent state. In this simple case, it is rather difficult for
the monitor data to be inconsistent, but in more complicated
situations, such as we shall encounter later, this is an important
consideration.

Another point to notice about the way in which *wait* is used is
that it appears within the control of an **if** statement, i.e. the Boolean
expression is tested once, and if the result is found to be true, the *wait*
is executed. The implication of this is that when the process is awoken

by a *signal* from another process at a later time, the procedure can continue and the Boolean expression of the **if** statement is not evaluated again. That is, when the *signal* is issued, it must only be in the situation where any one of the waiting processes can definitely be allowed to continue safely. A further implication is that any process which is waiting for a condition to be signalled must not be expected to compete with a newly arrived process attempting to make a fresh entry into the monitor, but must have priority treatment in re-entering the monitor, otherwise it would be possible for the waiting process to be signalled, and then the condition which caused the delay could be re-imposed by a new process before the waiting process could actually resume execution. Also, it is essential that the signalling

```
MonitorName:
     monitor
        begin

              { declaration of local variables }
              { including conditions }

              { declarations of local and }
              { visible procedures/functions }

              { initialisation statements }

        end; { monitor }
```
Program 4.6

process (i.e. the process which made the *signal* call) should leave the monitor immediately after the condition is signalled, in order to prevent the situation in which this process awakens a waiting process, and then itself alters the data and thereby re-imposing the circumstances which caused the signalled process to wait in the first place.

It is important to emphasise that, although the behaviour of a monitor condition variable would appear to be similar to that of a semaphore (and we may have enhanced this impression by using the same names for the operations acting upon them), there are two very significant differences between them. Firstly, the *wait* operation on a condition variable will always cause the calling process to suspend itself, unlike the semaphore *wait* which will decrement the semaphore counter and then only wait if the resulting value is negative. Thus, whereas the behaviour of a program using a semaphore will depend crucially upon the initial value given to the semaphore counter, a condition variable requires no initialisation. We have already noted that monitor conditions are frequently (in fact, almost always) associated with a Boolean expression which is generally tested before the wait is called, and this test in some sense replaces the test of the counter value during the semaphore wait operation.

The second, related, difference arises from the fact that a signal on a condition variable has no effect if no processes are waiting. Since there is no counter associated with a condition, it is not possible for *signal*s to "accumulate credit" which the *wait*s can subsequently "spend". Hence, if two processes A and B are expecting to co-operate by process A waiting for a signal from process B (by suitable calls to a monitor, of course), it is essential to ensure that process A should arrive at the *wait* before process B reaches the *signal*. If not, process B's attempt to signal becomes a null operation, and process A waits for ever, and hence is deadlocked. An example illustrating this problem, and a solution to it, are given in section 4.5.

Monitors, the general form of which is given as program 4.6, can vary according to the programming language in which they are defined, and we shall have more to say about languages which support concurrency in a later chapter, but the basic idea is the same. Some of the differences are to do with the extent to which the local variables of the monitor are visible to the outside world, and others restrict the procedures which are accessible to the users of the monitor. It may be desirable, for example, for users of the monitor to be able to interrogate the value of a variable within the data structure without the necessity for calling a function to achieve this. Some of the more liberal monitors may even allow variables to be changed without invoking the full power of the mutual exclusion imposed by the monitor, although this would appear to be inherently dangerous. On the more restrictive side, it may be felt necessary for only a subset of the procedures and functions defined within the monitor to be available to users of the monitor, and to allow the provider of the monitor to define procedures and functions for internal use only. In these latter cases, it is necessary for the syntax to provide a way of indicating which variables, procedures and functions are available to user processes. The initialisation statements are used to ensure that any necessary setting up of the local variables can be done before any process attempts to use the monitor.

4.4   Monitor Examples

Having looked at the general structure of a monitor and examined the facilities it offers, let us now look at some more examples of the use of monitors to solve certain problems in concurrent programming.

4.4.1   The Bounded Buffer

The first example to be considered is that of the *bounded buffer*. Recalling the discussion of the previous chapter and the previous section, we see that we need to provide mutual exclusion so that when any process is manipulating the buffer it is safe from interference by any other process, and also the buffer needs to be able to take appropriate action if an attempt is made to enter a new item into a full buffer, or remove an item from an empty buffer. As far as other processes are concerned, the way in which the buffer is implemented is of no concern, but some kind of specification of the external behaviour of the buffer is required. In this case, we can informally state that the properties of the buffer are that it offers a procedure *put*, which is called by the producer of an item, and a procedure (or function) *get*, which returns an item from the buffer either as a variable parameter or as the result to a calling consumer process. A sequence of calls on *get* will retrieve the items in the same order as they were presented to the buffer using *put*.

For the particular implementation which we will consider here, the buffer will be represented as an array *b* of elements of type *item*, together with a pair of indices *p* and *c* to act as pointers into the array and an integer valued variable *n* representing the number of items in the buffer at any given moment. Thus, the monitor can be written as in program 4.7. Since the buffer is bounded, there are two states of the buffer which will have a bearing on whether the operations *get* and *put* can be successfully carried out. It is clear that these two states are when the buffer is empty (i.e. when $n = 0$), in which case the *get* will be unable to succeed, and when the buffer is full (i.e. when $n = buffsize$), so that *put* will be unable to complete its operation. If we associate *condition* variables (*notfull* and *notempty*)

```
buffer:
      monitor
         begin
            const buffsize = ...;
                          { some appropriate value }
            var   b: array [0..buffsize-1] of item;
                  p, c: 0..buffsize-1;
                  n: 0..buffsize;
                  notfull, notempty: condition;

            procedure get (var m: item);
               begin
                  if n = 0 then notempty.wait;
                  m := b[c];
                  c := (c + 1) mod buffsize;
                  n := n - 1;
                  notfull.signal
               end;     { get }

            procedure put (m: item);
               begin
                  if n = buffsize then notfull.wait;
                  b[p] := m;
                  p := (p + 1) mod buffsize;
                  n := n + 1;
                  notempty.signal
               end;     { put }

            { initialisation code }
            p := 0; c := 0; n := 0
         end;     { monitor buffer }
```
Program 4.7

with each of these two states, we then have definitions for all of the local variables of the monitor.

It is unnecessary to describe the code in great detail, but one or two points need to be made. Firstly, the variable n will at all times contain the value of the number of full positions in the buffer, except of course when either of the procedures *get* or *put* is being executed. Assuming that the buffer contains both empty and full positions, the variables p and c represent, respectively, the first empty position and the first full position in the buffer. We observe here that, as a consequence of this particular method of implementation, there are two degenerate cases where p and c point at the same buffer slot. These two cases may be distinguished from one another by inspecting the value of n. Again, this statement is only true when the procedures are not actually in execution. These observations about the interpretation of the variables p, c and n represent consistency information concerning the state of the buffer, and the fact that they may not be true during the execution of the procedures is an indication of the necessity of the buffer procedures being critical sections of code, and hence being encapsulated within the monitor. The observation might also be made that the value of n can never go outside its stated bounds (0..*buffsize*), since within *get*, it can only be decremented if the conditional statement

if $n = 0$ **then** *nonempty.wait*

has been passed, which in turn can only happen if either the value of n was already greater than 0, or is signalled from the procedure *put* immediately following the incrementation of n. By a symmetric argument, n can never exceed the value *buffsize*.

The initialisation code of the monitor simply consists of the assignment of the value zero to n, indicating that the initial state of the buffer is empty, and initially the two pointers p and c have to point to the same buffer slot, slot zero being a convenient, but not essential, position to start.

The bounded buffer problem discussed in this section provides a simple example of the use of monitors, showing not only the necessity for mutual exclusion from critical parts of the code, but also the facilities available for processes to signal between themselves to indicate certain facts about the state of the shared data structure. Although it has more to do with the encapsulation of the data than the concurrency aspects *per se*, we may also observe that the user of the buffer is not required to know the details of the implementation of the buffer. It is sufficient for the monitor to advertise the routines which it makes available (and their purpose). If it were felt appropriate to alter the implementation of the bounded buffer, provided the externally visible procedures were not altered in appearance this could be done without alteration to (or even knowledge of) the client of the buffer.

4.4.2 The Readers and Writers Problem

In the next example we discuss, it is necessary to enhance the power of the monitor by associating an additional function with variables of type *condition*. The problem of the readers and writers was first posed by Courtois et al. and may be described as follows:

> A resource is to be shared amongst a number of concurrent processes so that some of the processes wish to access the resource without changing it, and others wish to alter the state of the resource. A convenient mental image is that of a file of data accessible by a number of user processes. On some occasions the file is to be read, which implies that it is not changed, and on other occasions the file is to be written, i.e. changed. The ground rules of the problem are that since the resource does not change state whilst being read, it may be read by any number of processes simultaneously. If any process is in the act of changing the state of the resource, then that process must have exclusive access to the resource, i.e. it would not be appropriate for another process either to be writing at the same time, or indeed reading while the writing was in progress.

In this problem, we require the use of a monitor to grant (or perhaps deny) access to the shared resource. In this sense, our monitor appears to be similar to the *SingleResource* monitor discussed earlier. However, in this case it is necessary for the user processes to indicate not only that they wish to use the resource, but also the mode in which they wish to do so. Thus the monitor must provide four operations (or procedures): *RequestRead*, *RequestWrite*, *ReleaseRead* and *ReleaseWrite*.

The internal variables of the monitor are almost as simple as the *SingleResource* case above, in that a Boolean is required to indicate whether or not the resource has been allocated exclusively to a process (i.e in response to a request to write). In addition, however, we require a variable to indicate whether or not the resource is being used for reading. Since more than one process may be in the act of reading the resource, this variable will have to be a counter rather than just a Boolean. Because there are two conditions under which a process may be delayed, namely an attempt to read and an attempt to write to the resource, it is necessary for the monitor to include two *condition* variables which will be named *oktoRead* and *oktoWrite*.

In designing a monitor to solve the readers and writers problem, or indeed in solving the problem by any method, a strategic decision has to be made. This may be stated as: If a number of processes are reading the resource and a request arrives to write to the resource, this request will be delayed. The question of strategy is to decide whether or not this request should take priority over subsequent read requests, which could in principle start immediately, since other reads are already in progress. The argument for allowing these requests to go ahead is that it maximises concurrency, or equivalently minimises the total delay. The disadvantage of this approach is that, in a heavily loaded system, the write operation may be delayed indefinitely. An additional disadvantage is that (presumably) a write request heralds the updating of the information held by the resource, and that delaying the write operation will mean that more reading of un-updated information will take place. The correct decision as to which of the two approaches to take will depend on the precise nature of the information held by the resource, and the frequency with which the resource is accessed.

This is the first example in which more than one condition variable appears, and a consequence of this fact is that in order to make strategic decisions such as the one discussed in the previous paragraph, it may be necessary to know whether or not there are processes waiting for a particular condition to be signalled. We therefore extend the definition of *condition* to allow the program to discover whether there has been an unsatisfied wait operation performed on the condition variable. Since we assume that condition variables may have queues associated with them indicating which processes are waiting on the condition, the additional operation takes the form of a function

ConditionName.queue

which returns the value *true* if there is at least one process waiting, and *false* otherwise.

```
ReadersAndWriters:
  monitor
    begin
      var readercount :    integer;
          writing     :    Boolean;
          oktoRead,
          oktoWrite   :    condition;

      procedure RequestRead;
      begin
        if writing or oktoWrite.queue then
                             oktoRead.wait;
        readercount := readercount + 1;
        oktoRead.signal
      end; { RequestRead }

      procedure ReleaseRead;
      begin
        readercount := readercount - 1;
        if readercount = 0 then
                             oktoWrite.signal
      end; { ReleaseRead }

      procedure RequestWrite;
      begin
        if writing or (readercount < > 0) then
                             oktoWrite.wait;
        writing := true
      end; { RequestWrite }

      procedure ReleaseWrite;
      begin
        writing := false;
        if oktoRead.queue then
                             oktoRead.signal
        else oktoWrite.signal
      end; { ReleaseWrite }

      { initialisation }
      readercount := 0; writing := false
    end; { monitor ReadersAndWriters }
```
Program 4.8

The solution to the readers and writers problem is now given as program 4.8 in which we see the four visible procedures together with the local variables discussed earlier. Taking the most straightforward procedure first, we observe that the procedure *RequestWrite* is very similar in form to *SingleResource.acquire*. The only difference is that it is necessary for the calling process to wait on the condition *oktoWrite* if writing is already in progress, or if there is any reading going on. In *ReleaseWrite* we see the use of the additional function associated with the type *condition*. We have chosen in this implementation to use the strategy in which the completion of a *write* operation will allow any queued *read* requests to be cleared before any *write* operations which may have been requested are started. In order to establish whether there are any such read requests, the value of *oktoRead.queue* is interrogated, and if the result is *true*, then there are outstanding *read* requests which are allowed to succeed through the *oktoRead.signal* statement. Otherwise one of the outstanding *write* requests (if there are any) is signalled.

The additional features of the *RequestRead* procedure are firstly that the calling process will be delayed if either another process is actually writing to the resource, or if there are other processes waiting to write. This again can be determined by calling the function *oktoWrite.queue*. Also, if a process is delayed in *RequestRead*, and then subsequently allowed to continue as the result of *oktoRead.signal*, it may be that other processes have been queued up behind the newly re-activated process, and these in turn can also be re-activated. This is the reason for the *oktoRead.signal* statement within the *RequestRead* procedure which essentially unblocks the whole queue of waiting processes rather than just the process at the head of the queue.

4.4.3   Disk-Head Scheduling

The final example of the use of a monitor introduces another extension to the facilities available through the *condition* mechanism. So far, we have said nothing about the way in which processes are handled when they are delayed by executing a *wait* statement on a condition. We have implicitly assumed that the scheduling is in some sense "fair", and by this we perhaps mean that signalling on a condition will awaken the process which has been in the waiting state on that condition for the longest time. For this last example, we introduce an extension which allows the programmer a limited amount of control over the scheduling of the processes which may be waiting for a signal.

The *wait* statement is extended to include a parameter which represents the priority of the process executing the *wait*. When a *signal* is executed, the waiting process with the highest priority is restarted. In fact, in this example, it is convenient to regard the *wait* statement executed with the lowest parameter value as having the highest priority.

The specific example concerns the scheduling of the arm of a disk unit according to the "lift" discipline. A typical magnetic disk attached to a computer system operates in the following manner (see figure 4.1):

Figure 4.1

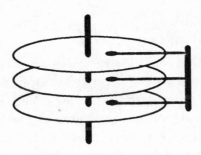

The information stored on the disk is organised into a series of *cylinders*, each of which consists of a number of *tracks*, and each track consists of a number of *sectors* or *blocks*. The unit has a single head carriage assembly which contains a read/write head for each track within a given cylinder, and the assembly is capable of aligning itself with a given cylinder. The disk itself is also rotating. In order to write new information on the disk, or to retrieve information already stored there, the sector address must be known, together with the track and cylinder numbers. The head assembly is moved to the correct cylinder, the head corresponding to the required track is selected, and the information may be read or written when the required sector passes the head as the disk rotates.

As far as this example is concerned, we are only interested in the cylinder numbers connected with each request, although a similar scheduling strategy could be applied to sector addresses within cylinders as well. However, the concern of this example is that it is generally undesirable for the head assembly to make random movements in order to position itself to process the requests in the order in which they arrive. It would be more efficient, and probably cause less mechanical strain on the device if the requests could be handled by making continuous sweeps across the disk surfaces, first in one direction and then in the other. The analogy with a lift in a building is that the lift will (usually) continue in one direction (either up or down) until there are no more requests to be satisfied by travelling in that direction, at which time it will begin to service the requests by travelling in the opposite direction. Also, a request for the use of the lift will be satisfied as the car reaches the point of the request, rather than in the chronological order in which the requests were made.

In designing a monitor to implement the scheduler using this policy, we require all of the facilities which have been introduced concerning the use of condition variables. The external appearance of the monitor consists merely of two procedures, and is similar to the *SingleResource* monitor, with the exception that the *request* procedure needs to be supplied with a single parameter indicating the cylinder for which the request is being made. Thus, calls will be made on this monitor in the form *DiskScheduler.request(cyl)* and *DiskScheduler.release*.

The internal structure requires the following variables, some of which have special significance with regard to the hardware device being controlled: *headpos*, reflecting the actual cylinder at which the heads are located at any given moment, *direction*, indicating the current direction of head movement, and *busy*, which is set to *true* whenever a request is being granted. The two possible values for *direction* are *up* and *down*, which are to be interpreted as meaning towards and away from the centre of the disk respectively. *Headpos* takes integer values in the range 0 to *MaxCyl*, the highest cylinder number, and an assignment to *headpos* represents the actual movement of the heads to the required cylinder. The requests are queued using the condition mechanism, and there will be two such conditions, one for the requests in each of the two possible directions of travel. Each request which is made when the disk is busy is queued on one of the condition queues, according to the requested cylinder number and its relation to the current position of the heads. When a

```
DiskScheduler:
  monitor
    begin
      type cylinder   =  0..MaxCyl;
      var headpos :    cylinder;
          direction :  (up, down);
          busy      :  Boolean;
          upsweep, downsweep  :   condition;

      procedure request (dest : cylinder);
      begin
        if busy then
          begin
            if (headpos < dest) or
               ((headpos = dest)
               and (direction = up)) then
                    upsweep.wait (dest)
               else downsweep.wait (MaxCyl - dest)
          end;
        busy := true; headpos := dest
      end; { request }

      procedure release;
      begin
        busy := false;
        if direction = up then
          begin
            if upsweep.queue then
                    upsweep.signal else
              begin
                direction := down;
                downsweep.signal
              end
          end else
            if downsweep.queue then
                    downsweep.signal else
              begin
                direction := up;
                upsweep.signal
              end
      end; { release }

      headpos := 0; direction := up; busy := false
    end; { monitor DiskScheduler }
```

Program 4.9

user process is successful in gaining access to the disk, it performs its reading or writing and then releases the disk using the procedure *DiskScheduler.release*. The code of the monitor appears as program 4.9.

4.5   A Cautionary Tale

Before we finally leave the subject of monitors, as we hinted in the previous discussion (section 4.4), we should show an example of the use of this form of concurrency control which might lead to unexpected results. Consider the concurrent program shown as program 4.10. Here, two processes, labelled *P1* and *P2*, attempt alternate accesses to the shared data structure represented by the monitor *M*.

The intention is that *P1* is required to *wait* (on condition *p*) until *P2* has completed some task, at which point it calls *M.go* to release *P1*. *P2* then waits until *P1* has performed its task, when it *signals* (condition *q*) to indicate that *P2* may continue. This program will apparently behave as intended, but there is the danger of deadlock occurring, and in practice, deadlock is almost guaranteed. We are not, it will be recalled, permitted to make any assumptions about the relative speeds of the processes *P1* and *P2*. Thus, either of the following sequences of events could occur:

(a)   Process *P2* reaches the call of *M.go* before *P1* attempts to call *M.stop*. Because of the monitor's mutual exclusion property, *P1* has to wait to enter the monitor. Suppose that *P2* is able to continue until it reaches the statement *q.wait*, which it may do since as yet no process is waiting on condition *p*. On reaching *q.wait*, *P2* relinquishes the monitor, *P1* enters and immediately waits on condition *p*, causing deadlock.

(b)   Even if *P1* is able to reach its monitor entry first, and halt at the call of *p.wait* in *M.stop*, the situation could arise in which process *P2* calls *M.go*, and thereby releases *P1*. The semantics of *signal* require, however, that *P2* leaves the monitor after performing *p.signal*, passing control to *P1*. *P1* then continues and will almost certainly reach the *q.signal* statement before *P2* has another chance to re-enter the monitor and execute its statement *q.wait*. Thus, a deadlock situation similar to that in (a) above results.

```
begin
    M:
      monitor
        begin
          var p, q : condition;

            procedure stop;
              begin
                p.wait;
                ...
                q.signal
              end; { stop }

            procedure go;
              begin
                ...
                p.signal;
                q.wait
              end; { go }

            { initialisation code }
          end;    { monitor M }

    cobegin

      P1:   begin
              ...
              repeat
                ...
                M.stop;
                ...
              until false
            end; { P1 }

      P2:   begin
              ...
              repeat
                ...
                M.go;
                ...
              until false
            end; { P2 }

    coend

end
```

Program 4.10

The principal cause of this undesirable effect is that *signal* behaves as a null operation when no process is waiting on the condition. By observing that in all our previous examples, condition variables were associated with Boolean expressions involving other components of the monitor data structure, we can create a solution to the problem posed in this section by modifying the monitor *M* as shown in program 4.11. Here we create a Boolean variable associated with each condition which "remembers" whether the signal has been called, and thus allows the process expecting the signal to discover whether it should wait for the signal, or whether the signal has already occurred.

This simple extension will solve the problem and avoid deadlock in the case where *two* processes communicate using the monitor *M*. If more processes wish to use the procedures *stop* and *go* (in some combination) it would be necessary to replace the Booleans

```
M:
    monitor
    begin
        var  p, q  :      condition;
             psignalled,
             qsignalled  :  Boolean;

    procedure stop;
        begin
            if not psignalled then p.wait;
            psignalled := false;
            ...
            qsignalled := true;
            q.signal
        end; { stop }

    procedure go;
        begin
            ...
            psignalled := true;
            p.signal;
            if not qsignalled then q.wait;
            qsignalled := false
        end; { go }

        { initialisation code }
        psignalled := false;
        qsignalled := false
    end; { monitor M }
```

Program 4.11

psignalled and *qsignalled* by counters which are incremented and decremented by the monitor procedures. In effect, we have recreated the semaphore machinery itself, relying on the monitor mechanism to provide the atomicity of the semaphore-style waiting and signalling.

4.6   Path Expressions

A monitor, as we saw in the previous sections, takes what might be described as an abstract data structure and imposes certain concurrency constraints upon the way in which the structure may be manipulated. All that the users of the monitor are aware of is the set of operations which are offered by the monitor, and none of the internal structure is visible. Since individual processes are not aware that they have been suspended (i.e. waiting on a condition), they cannot even know about the concurrency constraints. The mutual exclusion requirement is simply so that the operations of the abstract data type may be offered to multiple concurrent processes with no danger of the data structure being compromised by unwanted interference between concurrent users of the data structure.

In many cases, the total mutual exclusion constraint may be over-restrictive, in that it may be possible to determine that a particular pair (for example) of operations cannot interfere with one another because it can be demonstrated that they operate on different parts of the same structure. If a monitor is used to protect the integrity of the data structure, the two operations are mutually excluded despite the fact that no interference could occur. Such a situation can certainly arise in the example of the bounded buffer accessible to a single producer and a single consumer, where only an attempt to read and write *the same buffer slot* simultaneously will give rise to a conflict.

Campbell and Habermann's *path expressions* provide a way of specifying the concurrency constraints so that the abstract data type can be used more flexibly, and therefore more efficiently. Rather than simply to allow only one process into the monitor at a time, a path expression is associated with the data type specifying the concurrency constraints more explicitly. Path expressions also allow the specification of sequencing requirements as well as concurrency constraints. Finally, the path expression appears as part of the specification of the data object, so that the permitted modes of use of the data object are visible to each individual process and the collection of processes as a whole, without the need to understand the precise implementation details of the data object.

A path expression associated with an abstract data type must contain exactly one occurrence of each of the operations available to outside processes. (This could be considered as a method by which the data type informs the outside world which operations are being offered.) The operations are then related to one another using a set of connectors, and these connectors specify the concurrency and sequentiality requirements to be imposed on the use of the operations.

Assume we have an abstract data type offering operations a, b, c, etc. to allow concurrent processes to manipulate the structure. A *path* associated with an *object* of the type consists of the words **path** and **end** enclosing each of the names a, b, c, etc. (exactly once each) within the path. The path may be thought of as an iteration over the operations of the path in that when the path has been completed, it can begin all over again. Whilst within the path, however, the operations must be carried out according to the specifications of the path.

The operations may be connected in various ways, with perhaps the simplest example being a path with a single operation within it:

path a **end**

This simply means that the data object permits only one operation, a, which may be executed at any time, and to any desired level of concurrency. Similarly, no concurrency control is implied by the path:

path a, b, c, ... **end**

in which any of the operations a, b, c, etc. may be executed at any time. This includes the possibility that the operations may be executed by different processes concurrently.

A single operation may be restricted in the maximum number of concurrent executions by prefixing the operation with a constant number. Thus:

path 2: a **end**

constrains competing processes to a maximum of two simultaneous executions of the operation a. Parentheses may also be used to group together operations in a conventional way, which allows a path to be constructed to provide the effect of a monitor:

path 1: $(a, b, c, ...)$ **end**

In this example, the operations a, b, c, etc. may be executed in any order, but the maximum number of simultaneous executions of any operation or combination of operations is restricted to one, i.e. mutual exclusion is enforced by this path, making it functionally identical to a monitor.

Paths may also be used to impose sequentiality constraints upon the operations. This is designated by the use of a semi-colon between operation names. In the path

path a; b **end**

the operation a must precede the operation b. It is possible, however, for an arbitrary number of a operations to be in progress or have completed, but the sequentiality requirement is that no b operation may start until a corresponding a has completed. Thus the number of b operations either complete or in progress is always less than or equal to the number of completed a operations. We therefore have the notion that the path is in progress when either a or b is being executed, or when the path is "waiting at the semi-colon".

In conjunction with the concurrency limiting facility, we see that this construction allows us to provide a solution to the bounded buffer problem. Suppose a buffer object allowed concurrent processes to use the operations *put* and *get*, then we have two restrictions on the use of the buffer:

(a)   no more than *MaxBuff* (a constant) *put* operations may be performed without a corresponding *get* operation.

(b)   it is not possible to perform a *get* operation until the corresponding *put* has been executed.

These two restrictions are equivalent (respectively) to the condition which does not allow a *put* operation to take place if the buffer is full, and the condition which prevents a *get* operation being performed on an empty buffer. In the monitor example given in section 4.4, these two situations were represented by two condition variables within the monitor.

The view taken by the path object is that an attempt to remove an item from an empty buffer cannot occur if the path insists that a *get* operation must be preceded by a *put*, and that it is impossible for the full buffer problem to arise if operations on the buffer occur as *put/get* pairs, and that a maximum of *MaxBuff* such sequences are in progress at any time. Thus the path

path *MaxBuff*: (*put*; *get*) **end**

will achieve the desired effect. Up to *MaxBuff* invocations of the *put* operation may be attempted, but until one or more *get* operations are completed, the path will be still in progress, possibly delayed at the semi-colon, and therefore are constrained by the *Maxbuff* qualifier. Of course, if a *get* operation is completed, the number of *put/get* pairs in progress is reduced by one, making it possible for another *put* to be started.

The implementation of this buffer is of course more complex and may involve certain other concurrency constraints, and in particular, nothing has been said in the path concerning possible mutual exclusion of *put* and/or *get* operations. This whole problem will be discussed in greater detail in a later chapter, but it suffices at present merely to observe that the additional facilities of paths allow us to implement the bounded buffer without the use of condition variables. There are two main advantages to this approach over the monitor mechanism:

(a)   The path specification encapsulates the constraints on the buffer within the formal statement of the operation of the buffer.

(b)   The implementation of the buffer may be able to allow certain operations on the buffer to be carried out simultaneously provided it is satisfied that no problems will occur as a result. The monitor merely enforces mutual exclusion in the crudest possible form.

Paths may also be used to enforce the correct use of a single resource. The reader will recall that when discussing the monitor which controlled access to a single resource (section 4.3, program 4.5), it was necessary to assume that the user of the resource had correctly claimed (acquired) the resource before using it, and had correctly released it at the end. In fact, we assumed that processes would be sufficiently well-behaved that the operations which actually made use of the resource were not even included in the monitor. Provided the co-operating processes can be trusted, this does not matter. However, we can make this sequence of operations more secure by constructing an appropriate path. Suppose an object is available which represents a single resource, and which offers the operations *acquire*, *read* (and/or *write*) and *release*. A path can be written as:

path 1: (*acquire*; *read*; *release*) **end**

or:

path 1: (*acquire*; (*read*, *write*); *release*) **end**

In the first case, a process is not permitted to *read* until an *acquire* has been completed, and a *release* must be done following the *read* to complete the path and make it possible for a further *acquire* to take place. Similarly, in the second case, either a *read* or a *write* may be executed (but only one of them) provided an *acquire* has been executed previously, and a *release* must follow the reading or writing.

We should note that although this path mechanism prevents undesirable occurrences such as the use of the resource without its prior acquisition, it does not prevent a rogue process from using the resource when it has been acquired by another process. In order to prevent this type of fraudulent use of the resource, it is necessary for the implementation of the resource object to take note of the identity of the process which has successfully acquired it, and to allow only that process to make use of, and to release the resource.

In addition to the paths and path constructors described so far, there is an additional constructor which is particularly useful in the context of the Readers and Writers problem (see section 4.4.2). This is the so-called "burst" mode. An operation (or combination of operations) may be enclosed in square brackets as:

[*a*]

This is to indicate that if one instance of the operation *a* has begun, then others may also begin execution. This element of a path is considered to begin when the first such execution of *a* begins, and to terminate only when there are again no activations of *a*. It is clear that in order to solve the Readers and Writers problem, we would wish to constrain the operations on the resource to either a "burst" if *read*s or a single *write*. Thus, the required path is:

path 1: ([*read*], *write*) **end**

It should be noted that the use of the burst mode in this example does not allow the same measure of control over the scheduling of reads and writes as was possible in program 4.8. The path expression given above will give precedence to *read* operations, and will only allow a *write* to begin if there are no *read*s active. If any reading is taking place when another *read* is attempted, this latest operation will succeed, causing any pending *write*s to be delayed longer. In the case where the resource is being heavily used, this could easily result in a *write* operation being delayed indefinitely.

The main purpose of paths and path objects is to allow more flexibility in the concurrency constraints than is available using a monitor, and also to bring some of the hidden constraints, provided in a monitor by the condition variable mechanism, into a part of the object where such constraints may be stated explicitly as part of the external definition of the object. Path expressions thus allow the specification of these constraints to be separated from the implementation and free the user from the necessity of understanding the details of the implementation in order to determine the concurrency constraints. We shall discuss how paths may be mapped onto a suitable set of locking/controlling semaphores in chapter 7.

4.7   Exercises

4.1   Write a monitor to simulate the semaphore operations *signal* and *wait*.

4.2   Design a monitor solution to the Sleeping Barber problem (exercise 3.6).

4.3   Construct a solution to the Dining Philosophers problem (exercise 3.7) using one or more monitors. What can you say about your solution with respect to:
(a)   the degree of concurrency possible,
(b)   deadlock?

4.4   Modify the *SingleResource* monitor (program 4.5) so that it will control access to a fixed number N (> 1) of instances of a resource.

4.5   Design a monitor to handle the communication (i.e. provide a buffer) between a process which generates strings of characters and a process which takes the characters one at a time and displays them on a character-oriented output device. The monitor is required to offer two operations:
            PutString (s, n)
where s is a sequence of characters of length n, and:
            GetChar (c)
which returns a character in the variable c. It is also required to satisfy the usual buffering condition that the characters are taken out of the buffer in the same order as they were put in. The operation *PutString* should be delayed if there are less than n available character positions in the buffer, and *GetChar* will obviously be delayed if the buffer is empty.

4.6   Consider the behaviour of the monitor of exercise 4.5 in the case where there is more than one process calling the operation *PutString*. (We assume that it would be undesirable for the characters of a string from one process to be interleaved with the characters of a string from another process.)

4.7   The bounded buffer implemented as a single monitor as in program 4.7 is more restrictive (i.e. allows less concurrency) than it needs to. Consider ways in which the degree of permitted concurrency may be increased without compromising the integrity of the buffer data.

4.8   An implementation of the bounded buffer is proposed in which the buffer "owns" a pool of buffer slots, some of which contain messages, and some of which are "free". The pool of free buffer slots is organised as a linked structure, as is the list of full slots. Placing a message in the buffer consists of removing a slot from the pool of free slots, filling it with the incoming message, and attaching this slot to the tail of the list of full slots. Similarly, removing a message from the buffer consists of unlinking the slot at the head of this list, delivering the message to the caller and placing the (now free) slot back in the pool. Outline the implementation of such a buffer.

4.9   In the buffer of exercise 4.8, state the invariants of the implementation, and identify those points in the implementation where one or more invariants do not hold.

4.10   Given that the buffer of exercise 4.8 is implemented within a single monitor, it is clear that the points in the code where an invariant does not hold (as identified in exercise 4.9) will not affect the correctness of the behaviour. Consider ways in which the restrictions on concurrency imposed by a single monitor might be relaxed.

4.11   In section 4.4.2, the problem of the Readers and Writers is discussed, and an implementation given in program 4.8. It is also stated in the text that this solution implements one of the two strategies described. Show how you would modify program 4.8 to implement the alternative strategy.

4.12   In the disk head scheduling algorithm (program 4.9) it is possible for starvation to occur. State how this can happen, and give a simple alteration to the program which avoids this problem.

4.13   Programs 4.10 and 4.11 describe what might be termed a "stop/go" monitor to be used by a pair of co-operating processes. This enforces a discipline in which the process calling *stop* is held up until the other process calls *go*. It is also required that the "stop" process should signal to the "go" process to acknowledge the *go* operation. Consider how the monitor might be modified if more than two processes wished to participate in these interactions.

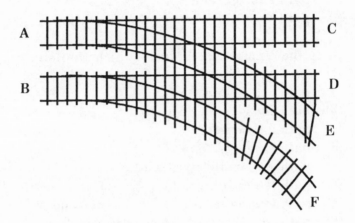

Figure 4.2

4.14   Figure 4.2 shows a simple railway junction. If we regard trains using the junction as processes, and the junction itself as a shared resource, a single resource monitor may be created which will prevent trains from colliding, provided only one train is permitted access at a time, and assuming that trains do not attempt to use the junction without obtaining permission.

By considering the journey which a train wishes to make through the junction, it may be possible to allow more than one train into the junction simultaneously. Write a monitor which offers the operations *acquire* (*to, from*) and *release* (*to, from*) which controls the junction safely and yet allows maximal concurrency.

4.15   Describe in words the constraints (if any) imposed by the following Path Expressions:

    (a)   **path** a **end.**

    (b)   **path** a, b, c **end.**

    (c)   **path** $a; b; c$ **end.**

    (d)   **path** 1: (a) **end.**

    (e)   **path** 5: (a) **end.**

    (f)   **path** 1: $(a), b$ **end.**

    (g)   **path** 1: (a), 1: (b) **end.**

    (h)   **path** 1: (a, b, c) **end.**

    (i)   **path** 3: $(a, 2: (b))$ **end.**

4.16   State the circumstances under which the following Path Expressions would be used:

    (a)   **path** put, get **end.**

    (b)   **path** $put; get$ **end.**

    (c)   **path** 1: (put, get) **end.**

    (d)   **path** 1: $(put; get)$ **end.**

    (e)   **path** 5: (1: (put); 1: (get)) **end.**

    (f)   **path** 1: $(put, [get])$ **end.**

    (g)   **path** 1: $(acquire; (read, write); release)$ **end.**

    (h)   **path** $(acquire; (read, write); release)$ **end.**

5
High-Level Concurrency
Constructs - Message Passing

All the high-level constructs discussed in the previous chapter have been of the "shared data" form. By this we mean that processes wishing to communicate with each other do so not by addressing one another directly, but by accessing data which is known and available to them all. The constructs also provide ways of accessing the shared data which ensure that the data itself is not compromised by undesirable simultaneous accesses by competing processes by offering operations in the form of procedures and functions to control the manipulation of the data. The data structure itself is purely passive, and changes are made to the structure by allowing procedures and functions to be called by the active elements in the system, namely the processes. As these procedures are called, they in a sense become part of the process which calls them, and the data itself temporarily becomes part of the address space of the calling process. We could also use the term "procedure oriented" to describe this view. We observe that the competing processes are not required to have any knowledge of the identities of their competitors, but merely to know the name of the object(s) they wish to access, and which operation(s) they wish to apply to the data.

By contrast, we shall now discuss a different class of techniques for allowing concurrent processes to communicate with each other. We shall see later how the two approaches can be considered as analogous to each other. The view we now wish to examine is known as the "message-passing" approach, and we shall see later that it would also be appropriate to describe the approach as "process oriented". In this class of techniques, each process has its own self-contained state space, or address space, which is not shared by any other process either as a whole or in part. The mechanism by which data is passed from one process to another is through some kind of message-passing technique. It would of course be quite possible to implement a message-passing mechanism using a shared data structure, as we have already seen, but we now wish to consider the message-passing operations as being primitives which are part of the underlying architecture providing concurrency support, and are available to any process wishing to use them.

5.1   Simple Message Passing

The simplest form of interaction between two processes *P1* and *P2* is for one of them (say *P1*) to send a message to the other (without *P2* replying; the reliability of the message transfer mechanism is not in question). For this to occur, *P2* must call the primitive *receive*, and *P1* must call *send*, specifying both the message to be sent and the intended recipient (*P2*). Thus it is necessary for *P1* to be aware of *P2*'s identity. In this simple example it is not necessary for *P2* to be aware of the identity of *P1*, not even after the message has been delivered. In this case, the two operations required may be represented by the following Pascal procedure headings:

procedure *send* (*p* : *ProcessId*; *m* : *MessageFormat*)

and:

procedure *receive* (**var** *m* : *MessageFormat*)

We suggested above that we do not wish to question (at present) the reliability of the mechanism which carries out the transfer of the message. For the transfer actually to take place, there must be a degree of synchronisation between the communicating processes. Precisely what this synchronisation entails is a matter for the implementor of the underlying system, particularly as the individual processes are supposedly unaware of the passage of time if for any reason they are unable to make progress. Thus the semantics of the operation *send* are that the procedure is complete when the message has ceased to be the responsibility of the sending process. If the process should happen to be delayed for any reason while attempting to send a message, the process will not be aware of the delay. Similarly, the process wishing to receive a message will be delayed until a message is available. Having called the *receive* primitive, the process will not be aware of any further progress until the *receive* completes by delivering the incoming message.

The implications of this discussion are that the sending and receiving processes may be required to synchronise absolutely in order to transfer a message, meaning that a *send* must wait until a matching *receive* is also invoked, after which the message transfer takes place, and the two processes can continue along their separate execution paths. Alternatively, the underlying system may be capable of buffering messages, in which case an attempted *send* will complete as soon as the buffer mechanism has taken the message and placed it in its own private memory space ready for delivery when an appropriate *receive* call is made.

Since the sending and receiving processes are unaware of any delays there may be within the message transfer mechanism, distinctions such as these are of no interest to the communicating processes. There are, however, variations of the message transfer mechanism which are of interest to, and may have consequences for, the users of the *send* and *receive* primitives.

5.2   The Client/Server Model

Although in our simplest example we assumed that the receiving process had no knowledge of, nor interest in, the source of the received message, it is very common for the receiving process to need to know where the message came from. A possible example might be when a process is offering a service of which a number of processes (called *clients*) may wish to avail themselves. Typically, the process offering the service (called a *server*) will need to carry out an action on behalf of a client, and then reply to the client indicating the result(s) of the action. In such circumstances, it is clearly necessary for the server to know the identity of the client, since it could be any one of a number of clients who requested the service. A simple modification to the *receive* operation will make this possible:

procedure *receive* (**var** *p: ProcessId*; **var** *m : MessageFormat*)

The two procedures *send* and *receive* as defined so far represent the simplest possible mechanism for passing messages between processes. Any synchronisation which may take place as a result of passing messages is not significant as far as the component processes are concerned. There are however some possible alterations which may be made to the message system which do affect the behaviour (and not just the timing) of the communicating processes.

In the procedure *receive* as it appears above, the calling process is given the first message which was sent to that process. If for any reason, the process wishes to receive a message from a specified sender, then the receiving process must take responsibility for accepting all of the messages sent to it, and dealing with them at a later time. (This responsibility might take the form of simply replying to the sender of each unwanted message, asking for the message to be sent again at a later time.) When the awaited message arrives, the receiver can take the required action and then return to the problem of the messages which arrived in the interim (or waiting for them to be resubmitted).

It is possible for the message system to handle this on behalf of the processes, however, by allowing the user of the *receive* primitive the option of specifying the process from which a message is to be received. Clearly it would not be desirable for this to be the only way of receiving messages, but in some instances it would be more convenient for the system to handle the queuing of unwanted messages rather than placing this responsibility with the user process.

We have already introduced the notion of two processes being in client/server relationship to one another, and in general, clients will expect some kind of reply to their requests for service. Consider the situation shown in figure 5.1. Process *P3* is a server which offers services, and let us assume that *P1* and *P2* are typical clients of *P3*. It is frequently the case that the server process *P3*, while processing a request from a client (say *P1*), discovers that it itself wishes to make a request for service from another server *P4*. The process *P3* is therefore

Figure 5.1

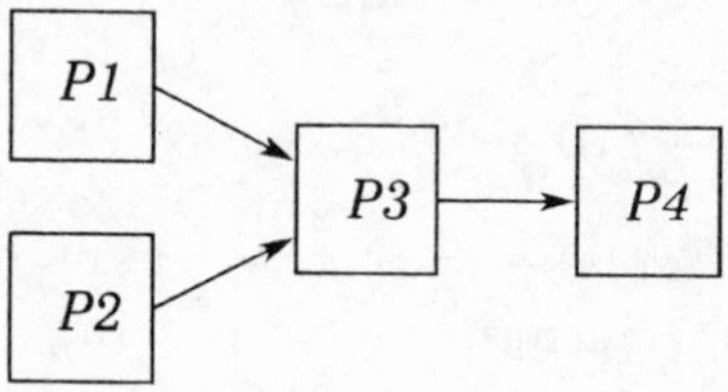

acting both as a client and as a server at the same time. Suppose now that *P3*, in processing a request from *P1*, sends a message to *P4*. It will be unable to complete the service for *P1* until a reply is received from *P4*, and would therefore call the *receive* procedure. If this procedure simply accepted the next message to be sent to *P3*, then the message received might be coming from anywhere such as a new client *P2*. If this occurred, *P3* would have to remember the message from *P2* and process it at a later stage, or else send a reply to *P2* asking for the message to be resubmitted later.

5.3   The Selective *receive*

A better solution to this problem would be to allow the process *P3* to make what is effectively an "inter-process procedure call". That is, *P3* "calls" a service offered by *P4* by sending a message to *P4* and waiting for a reply also from *P4*. There is then no danger of a message from a process such as *P2* interfering with the processing of the request from *P1*. This example demonstrates a situation in which it would be advantageous for a process to specify the process from which it wishes to receive a message.

If we admit that a user of the *receive* primitive within a message-passing system is permitted to specify one process from which the next message is to come, why should we not allow that user to specify a *set* of processes, one of which is to be the source of the next message? The most general form of *receive* would be to give the caller of the receive procedure the opportunity to specify that it wishes to receive the next message from any one of a subset of the possible processes (of which the whole set is of course a special case). A possible application would be the case where a server process might wish to restrict its clients, for reasons of security or safety of the whole system, to a subset of the processes in the system.

A restrictive special case of the selective *receive*, which also offers an alternative mechanism for providing the inter-process procedure call facility discussed earlier, is to extend the message system to include a *reply* primitive. This operation looks like a *send*, but is only used following a *receive* to acknowledge that the message has been delivered. The *send* itself must then be modified so that the sending process is blocked until the *reply* is received. The unconstrained *send* and *receive*, and the send with blocking until the reply is received are illustrated in figure 5.2(a) and (b). In both of these diagrams, we have shown the *receive* being executed before the *send*, i.e. the receiving process has to wait until the send primitive is called by the sending process. The situation in which the send occurs before the receive is illustrated in figure 5.3(a) and (b). Notice that in figure 5.3(b), the sending process is delayed for two reasons; firstly because the receiving process is not ready to accept the message, and then because the reply has to be returned before the sender can continue. The first of these delays would be less likely to occur if the message system included a message buffer.

5.4   Process Identities and the Name Server

In all the examples of message passing described in the previous sections, reference has been made by processes to the identity of another process with which communication is taking place. In high-level language terms, this implies that a data type *ProcessId* should exist and be available to all the processes. There are a number of interesting issues involved in the way in which a process obtains the identity of another process with which it wishes to communicate.

The simplest way in which this can be done is to allow the process identifiers to be known globally throughout the whole of the concurrent program. Thus, if process *A* wishes to send a message to process *B*, then the identifier *B* is known to the program running as process *A* and can be used as an argument in a *send* call. The symmetric situation is that process *B* knows that the message will come from *A*, and can reply, if required to, by sending a message back to *A*.

Only slightly more complex is the client/server situation discussed in section 5.2, in which the client (say *A*) knows that it wishes to obtain a service from the server (*B*), but *B* may receive requests for service from any one of a number of possible client processes. Process *A* therefore uses the opportunity of sending a message to inform *B* that *A* is the sender, and that the reply should therefore be returned to *A*.

Facilities such as these are available within the existing set of message-passing primitives, in that the type *ProcessId* is specified to be the type of one of the parameters of *send* and/or *receive*. We have said nothing so far in this section or the previous one about the content

Figure 5.2(a): Unconstrained Send

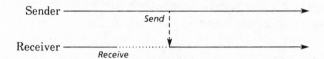

Figure 5.2(b): Send Blocked until Reply

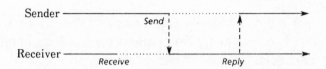

Figure 5.3(a): Unconstrained Send

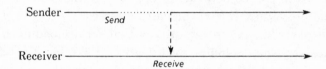

Figure 5.3(b): Send Blocked until Reply

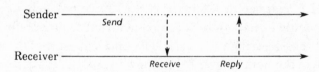

of the message itself. The actual interpretation of the message contents is obviously a matter for agreement between the communicating processes, but it would be an advantage if our message transport mechanism would be willing to carry messages of arbitrary types, and in particular, that the messages could be structured according to any convenient record structure mutually agreed between the processes. If, in addition, it was agreed that values of type *ProcessId* could themselves be contained in a message structure, then the way would be open for a much more flexible interaction between the various processes in the system.

Using these notions, it is now possible to introduce the concept of a *name server*. This is a process to which messages may be sent in order to ascertain the identity of the process to which the real request should be sent. As an example, suppose a client process wishes to make use of services offered by a data base server *DB*. The client would not have necessarily to remember the identity of *DB*, but could send a request to the name server (*NS*) which says "please tell me the identity of the data base server". The name server may now reply "the data base server you require can be accessed using the identity *DB*". The client is now able to communicate with *DB* without any further interaction with *NS*.

This approach has a number of advantages. Firstly, there may be good reasons why the system administrator may wish to change the identity of a particular process. If clients observe the protocol given above in order to access the services they require, then the system administrator is free to alter the identity of any process, and the only change required is one adjustment to the information stored in the name server. The alternative is that all processes wishing to access another service would have the identity of that service bound in, and all such processes would require modification if the identity of the service were to be changed. There may, of course, be transient situations in which a process has asked the name server for the identity of a server process, and during the lifetime of the subsequent interaction with that server, its identity may have to be changed. In such cases, it would be necessary to intercept all subsequent references to the server process during the interaction, and request that the client enquire again of the name server for the new identity of the server.

Another advantage of the name server approach is when the service could be provided by any one of a number of (nearly) identical servers. For instance, suppose a client wished to send information to a printer, and suppose also that there were several printers available, each with its own driver process. The client may not be concerned which of the printers is to be used to satisfy his request, so that an additional function of the name server could be to provide the identity of one of a number of possible servers, according to which one of them was available. Hence, the client sends a message to the name server asking "please tell me the identity of a (any) printing server" to which the name server might reply "use *PS2*", knowing that *PS2* is free, whereas *PS0* and *PS1* may not be. The name server may have this knowledge stored in its own tables, implying that all use, and indeed the termination of use, must be communicated back to the name server (in which case it becomes a *resource manager* as well as a name server). Alternatively, the name server could temporarily switch from being a server to being a client, and issue the request "are you busy?", to each printing server, and reply to the original client with the identity of the first printer driver to reply with "No, I am not busy".

The name server could also act as a filter which monitors requests for new processes to be made available. Thus, we might postulate that a process manager *PM* is responsible for creating new processes and making them available for use as child processes to an existing process. Again, the name server could be asked to provide the identity of a new process, and the name server returns the identity of such a process after suitable negotiations with *PM*.

The final advantage of the name server mechanism is that the client only has to be aware *a priori* of the identity of the name server itself. All other information concerning the identity of processes can be obtained from *NS* by suitable requests. Of course, in order for such an arrangement to work satisfactorily, the client processes must be aware of:

(a)   the messages required to identify the required server from the
        name server,

and

(b)   the identity of the name server itself.

It follows from this that the identity of the name server must be a *well-known* ProcessId, and must therefore be chosen with great care, since the consequences of having to change it are quite extensive.

5.5   Channels, Mailboxes and Pipes

As an alternative to making the identities of processes known to other processes, either by making the names globally known, or by providing the facilities of a name server so that messages may be sent directly to one or more receiving processes, some systems of concurrency view the communication channel itself as the named entity by which information is passed. Thus, instead of specifying that process *A* wishes to send a message to process *B*, the same effect could be achieved by process *A* asking to send a message through channel *C*. Process *B* could then request a message from channel *C*, and process *A*'s message would be delivered.

The programming language OCCAM, which we shall examine at greater length in the next chapter, has a very static concurrency structure, and all communication between the concurrent components takes place via channels. These channels must be declared in such a way that all the processes which need to use them are within the scope of the declaration. It is not possible in OCCAM to communicate using a channel unless that channel is known to the process in advance, i.e. at compile time. Although it is not of concern to the concurrent processes themselves, communication in OCCAM also has the feature that it is synchronous, in the sense that the processes may only carry out the transfer of information along a channel when a sender and a receiver are both attempting to communicate by referring to the same channel. Thus there is a high degree of synchronisation between communicating processes in the language.

Despite the rigidity of the channel mechanism, a kind of client/server relationship can still be established, but the client is required to know not only the method by which requests may be sent to the server, i.e. the channel on which the server receives requests, but also the channel on which the reply will be delivered. Then the server can send its replies to a known, fixed channel which is also known to the waiting client. There is a danger in such a mechanism, however, that a reply could be sent to the wrong process. That is, if a client CL sends a message to a server, it is possible that when the client asks to read from the reply channel, another process is already waiting, which will receive the reply intended for CL. Although such erroneous behaviour is a possibility, if all processes use the server properly, and wait for the reply as soon as they have delivered the request, then the incorrect reception of replies would appear to be unlikely, though not impossible.

The inflexibility of the process and channel structure in OCCAM appears to preclude the creation of a name server process, but it would be possible for requests for service to be sent to the name server which forwards them directly to the server concerned. This is not an attractive solution, in that the name server now becomes a "service switch", and the problems of keeping track of where messages should be sent, and the correct destination of the replies, seems to mitigate against the elegance of the name server concept, and to remove much of the functional separation which is a major benefit of concurrency.

The language Pascal-m is an extension of Pascal which includes entities called *mailboxes*. Mailboxes are typed channels to which messages may be sent, and from which messages may be received. They behave in very much the same way as the buffers which we programmed explicitly using monitors and path objects in the previous chapter. The type of a mailbox defines the structure of the messages which it may contain. Unlike OCCAM channels, values of type *mailbox* may be passed around, and in particular, they may be sent as part of a message into and out of other mailboxes. Thus, it becomes very simple both to provide the client/server system, where the server makes known the identity of the mailbox by which it will receive requests for service, and the client can send, as part of a request, the mailbox by which the reply is to be delivered. It also becomes trivial to create a name server, in which servers can be accessed not by telling the name server their own process identification, but by giving the name server the identity of the mailbox by which they can be contacted.

The mailbox scheme has a slight advantage over the straightforward mechanism of referring to a process by name, in that a process can request services from a number of different servers, and can control the order in which the replies are processed, by declaring a number of mailboxes through which the replies will be returned. Each separate request can then indicate a separate reply mailbox, and thus the client issues *receive* operations from the reply mailboxes in any order it wishes. If, on the other hand, the client does not care about the order in which the replies are received, then it can pass the same mailbox to each server process, and take the replies in whatever order they happen to be generated.

5.5.1 UNIX Pipes

Similar to the mailbox is the construct offered by the UNIX system called a *pipe*. Unlike Pascal-m's mailboxes however, which are structured data types allowing particular operations to be performed on them, and which will receive and deliver messages of a particular declared type, pipes are intended to appear as input/output devices. In keeping with the UNIX tradition that all input/output operates only on sequences of bytes, so only sequences of bytes may be passed through a pipe.

The actual mechanism available to the UNIX programmer is a system call to create the pipe, which then may be "inherited" by a child process subsequently created as a result of the *fork* system call. This then enables the parent process and the child to communicate with one another by writing to and reading from the pipe. Although, following the fork operation, the parent and child processes have access to the pipe for both reading and writing, this is an inherently risky method of operating, since the non-determinism of the system means that it is possible for a process to write to the pipe, and then read back its own message! If two-way communication is required, then the recommended method is to create two pipes, one for parent-to-child communication, and one for message passing in the reverse direction. Pipes are of course inherited by *any* child process forked after the pipe is created, and thus two (or more) children of the same parent may use pipes to communicate with one another.

Another important difference between pipes and mailboxes arises out of the fact that the data which passes through a UNIX pipe, as with all UNIX input/output, is a sequence of bytes, whose length is specified at the time of writing to, or reading from, the pipe. This contrasts with the mailbox approach, which allows only a single message (but which may have an almost arbitrarily complex structure) to be inserted into, or taken out of, the mailbox on each *send* or *receive* call. In a mailbox system, therefore, any attempt to take a message from a mailbox will always succeed unless the mailbox is completely empty. Pipes, on the other hand, may contain some data, and yet be unable to satisfy a particular read request. The UNIX *read* call takes, as one of its parameters, the number of bytes to be transferred. The value returned by the call is the actual number of bytes transferred, which may or may not be the same as the parameter. In the operation of a pipe, if the pipe is completely empty, then a process attempting to *read* from the pipe is delayed (i.e. put to sleep), whereas if the pipe contains one or more bytes, the *read* call succeeds, but returning as many bytes as are available up to the total number required as specified by the parameter of the call.

The behaviour of the pipe on writing is somewhat simpler, in that a *write* operation will only succeed when all of the bytes to be transferred have been accepted by the pipe, and this may mean that the writing process is delayed until another process has removed some bytes. The exception to this behaviour is when a *write* request asks to transfer more bytes than the maximum capacity of the pipe, in which case, the *write* request succeeds, but returns a value equal to the total number of bytes actually transferred.

5.5.2 Named Pipes

It is clear that, although the pipe will indeed provide a facility for two (or more) UNIX processes to pass messages to one another, the fact that a pipe can only be inherited by children of the pipe's creator limits the use of this style of pipe very considerably. For example, it is not possible for a pipe to be used as the communication channel by which an arbitrary client may communicate with a pre-existing server process. The difficulty arises because when a pipe is created, it is also opened, and when it is closed, it is destroyed. What is required is a mechanism whereby a pipe can exist even though it is not opened for use. A mechanism by which this may be achieved is through *named pipes*. In systems supporting named pipes, one of the system calls will allow the creation of a name within the file system hierarchy specifying that this name refers to a pipe. Any process may then attempt to open the pipe, using the standard *open* system call, either for reading or for writing. In order for the pipe to be used, there must be at least one process which has successfully opened the pipe for writing, and at least one for reading. When this has occurred, a conversation can take place using the pipe. If a process attempts to open the pipe for reading (or writing) when there is no corresponding process opening the pipe for writing (or reading), then the process just waits (i.e. sleeps) until a process comes along and tries to open the pipe for the appropriate type of use. Once the named pipe is open, then the pipe is used by the participating processes in the same way as unnamed pipes are used.

Closing a pipe (either named or unnamed) will also have an effect on other processes involved in the use of the pipe. Clearly, as long as there is at least one process reading and writing the pipe, then communication is possible, so the pipe remains open. However, as soon as the number of readers or writers reduces to zero, the pipe ceases to be available for inter-process communication, and we have to describe how other processes behave in this case. Let us consider first what happens if the number of writers becomes zero. All outstanding *read* requests (i.e. processes sleeping waiting for data to become available) are awoken, and the *read* calls returned with an indication that no data has been read. (This is equivalent to the end-of-file indication when reading from a file.) All subsequent *read* attempts also return with zero bytes having been transferred. If, as a result of a *close* request, the number of readers reduces to zero, then any process waiting to write to the pipe is awoken, and a UNIX *signal,* or *exception,* is sent to the process. This would be a somewhat unusual situation, since the fact that a *write* call puts the process to sleep means that the pipe is full, and yet the last reader has closed the pipe.

5.5.3   UNIX Messages

Two versions of UNIX have incorporated additional facilities for inter-process communication. The first is the so-called System V, which provides a genuine inter-process message-passing capability. Messages may be of arbitrary type, and in fact different message types may be passed along the same message channel. The messages are stored in a linked list, thus ensuring (unlike the pipe) that each message can be regarded as a separate entity. (It is clearly important that the recipient of each message has enough information about each incoming message to be able to retrieve the message and to interpret it correctly.) Message channels are accessed by calling a system function named *msgget,* one of whose parameters is an identifier for the channel. Another parameter provides the calling process with some additional control over the action of the get operation, including, for example, the ability to create new channels. The channel identifier may then be given to other processes so that they too can make use of the message channel. The *msgget* call returns a descriptor for the message channel, which is then used in subsequent attempts to send or receive messages.

By contrast with the pipe, a message channel passes objects with more structure than a simple sequence of bytes, and thus it would not be appropriate for the usual *read* and *write* system calls to be used. System V therefore provides *msgsnd* and *msgrcv* system calls by which processes can use the message passing facilities. These of course have to take the descriptor returned by *msgget* as one of their parameters.

Although before using a message channel it is necessary for a process to obtain a descriptor, which of course requires a call to *msgget*, the actual identifier of the channel may be chosen by the user. Since the channel identifier is actually an integer value, it can presumably be passed from one process to another, and in this way the means by which commonly required services may be accessed can be communicated from one process to another. Thus, it is clearly straightforward to use this mechanism to provide the facilities of a server.

5.5.4 Sockets

The BSD4 series of UNIX systems, written by the University of California at Berkeley, adopted a different approach to the problem of inter-process communication, in which it was recognised that it would be useful to be able to communicate not only with processes within the same system, but also with processes in other UNIX (and possibly non-UNIX) systems, running on different machines, and connected by a communications network.

It is not our intention here to discuss the problems of communicating over networks, but to describe how these facilities may be used for inter-process communication within a single system.

BSD UNIX offers the programmer a system call named *socket*, which essentially creates an "opening" through which communication may take place. In making a *socket* call, the process must specify a *domain* within which this inter-communication will take place. This is primarily used to specify a family of communication protocols to be used over the network, but one of the options is the UNIX domain. Having created a socket, the process must then *bind* the socket to an *address*, the form of which depends on the domain to be used. In the case of the UNIX domain, this address has the form of a UNIX filename.

A process wishing to communicate with another process will make the system call *connect*, specifying the address of the intended correspondent. This call will clearly fail if the specified address does not exist, or if no process is ready to receive a connection request naming this address. A server process will indicate its willingness to establish connections by issuing the call *listen* on a socket which has already been opened and bound to a well-known address. Processes wishing to avail themselves of the facilities of the server must then connect their own socket to this well-known address. The *listen* call returns when a connection request is received, and will then call the function *accept*. This will return with a new socket descriptor which will then be used for the conversation with the client, whose connect call will return when the conversation is properly set up. The creation by the server of a new socket as a result of the accept call allows the server to fork a new process to handle the client's request, and to return itself to its own main loop, where it can listen on the original socket for further service requests.

Once the conversation has been established, the data transferred is once again simply a sequence of bytes, and hence standard *read* and *write* system calls can be used. The socket mechanism also has a *send* and a *recv* system call, and these may take an additional parameter in order to take advantage of certain other facilities offered by sockets. These are primarily concerned with network communications, and as such are beyond the scope of this book.

5.6   Channels and Guarded Commands

In chapter 2, we saw how the guarded commands of Dijkstra could be used to introduce and control non-determinacy. The guards which were introduced then were merely Boolean expressions, and we saw how, within a parallel construct, any one of the guarded commands whose guard evaluated to true *could* execute. The choice of which one *would* execute was indeterminate. The iteration construct allowed for the possibility of *each* guarded command with a true guard would execute eventually.

In Hoare's Communicating Sequential Processes, or CSP, the notion of a guard and a guarded command are extended to include input and output guards. While Dijkstra's guards are simple Boolean expressions, and therefore can be immediately evaluated to either a true or false result, the input and output guards of CSP may have a third state, which we shall call *pending*.

The general form of the CSP-style guard is:

<Boolean expression> & <i/o guard>

where the <i/o guard> is of the form:

$$c?v \quad \text{or} \quad c!e$$

and either (but not both) of the components of a guard may be empty, and if the <Boolean expression> is not present, a true value is assumed.

The two <i/o guard> constructs represent communication between processes in CSP, and the notion of information passing into or out of a process from or to its environment suggests that *input/output* is an appropriate description of these constructs. The construct $c?v$ describes the operation of accepting a value on channel c, and assigning that value to the variable v. The construct $c!e$ causes the evaluation of the expression e, the result of which is delivered on the channel c. Neither of these two constructs can complete until another parallel process is ready to match up with the input/output operation requested. Thus, the i/o guard $c?v$ will remain pending until there is a parallel process attempting to perform an output operation specifying the same channel c.

The value of the guard is then:

false - if the <Boolean expression> evaluates to *false*.

true - if the <Boolean expression> evaluates to *true*, and the input/output component of the guard (if present) is able to complete.

pending - if the <Boolean expression> evaluates to *true*, but the <i/o guard> is awaiting a matching input/output statement which has not yet occurred.

CSP was first presented as a theoretical approach to the problem of communication between concurrent statements, complementing and enhancing the non-determinacy introduced by guarded commands. It has now become a language, and has acquired an implementation in its own right. However, we shall also observe how guarded commands, including input/output guards, have influenced the development of the two high-level languages ADA and OCCAM. In the next chapter we shall see how the ADA *rendezvous* construct is used to allow concurrent processes (or *tasks*, as they are called in ADA) to communicate with one another using a form of message passing, and also how OCCAM uses a channel concept very similar to that of CSP to pass messages between components operating in parallel.

5.7   On Message Passing and Shared Data

In this chapter we have examined inter-process message passing as a means of communication, and contrasted it with the shared data approach considered in the previous chapter. It is worth spending a short while comparing these two approaches.

We can in fact take the two styles, and, almost mechanically, transform a program written in one style to an equivalent program in the other. It is clear that if we begin with the message passing form, all that is required is to provide a message buffer which is shared by both parties to the communication. There are a number of issues associated with this transformation which concern themselves with the various styles of message passing discussed in the earlier section of this chapter. Channels and mailboxes are clearly the simplest forms from the point of view of this transformation, since the channel/mailbox name can be offered to the parallel processes taking part in the interaction. This is modelled in the shared data style by creating a (bounded) buffer whose identity can also be offered to the communicating processes.

When the interaction takes place by the sending process naming the receiving process explicitly, it becomes necessary to create a message buffer related to the receiving process into which messages destined for that process may be placed. The situation becomes even more constrained if the *receive* primitive is permitted to nominate the source process of the message. In this case, it will be necessary to create a separate message buffer for each pair of processes wishing to communicate, and indeed, one such buffer is required for each direction of message transfer.

Suppose now we have a program which has been written using the shared data style of process interaction. In particular, we shall assume that the monitor construct is used to represent a typical interaction of this type. We postulate that it is possible to create an equivalent program, in which each monitor is replaced by an additional process to act as the "manager" of the data protected by the monitor. (We note here that, in providing such a manager, we are assuming that the data which was previously shared between the processes has now been identified, and encapsulated as the "private" data of the new manager process.) Whenever a process in the shared data version calls a monitor procedure, this is replaced in the message passing model by a message passed to the manager process, followed by a receive operation, awaiting a reply from the manager process. The message to be sent consists of an indication of the function to be carried out by the manager process - corresponding to the name of the monitor procedure to be called, together with the parameters for the call. The calling process is thus suspended, as it would be while waiting for a monitor procedure to complete, and the manager carries out the required task, corresponding to executing the code of the procedure body. On completion of the task, the manager sends an acknowledgement to the calling process, together with any results which might be appropriate, which releases the calling process to continue executing.

The mutual exclusion required by the monitor is assured since the manager will complete the processing associated with one message before accepting the next. In this sense, the message-passing mechanism replaces the need for queuing at the entry to a monitor. If a process is forced to wait on a condition, this corresponds to the manager process delaying its reply to the calling process, and accepting other requests, until the circumstances permit the completion of the operation requested. This could, of course, imply the maintaining of a queue for each condition variable in the original monitor.

We give a simple example to illustrate this transformation. Suppose we wish to construct a concurrent program to solve the producer/consumer (bounded buffer) problem. For simplicity, we shall assume that there is only one producer and one consumer. We shall also assume that the message passing takes place by specifying the destination process and the message when sending, and that receive will accept messages from any process, returning both the message and the identity of the source process. We do not require any assumptions about the underlying *send* and *receive* mechanism with regard to whether it is synchronous or asynchronous.

buffer: **monitor** ...   { as in program 4.7 }

cobegin

producer: **repeat**
     producemessage (m);
     buffer.put (m)
  until *false*;

consumer: **repeat**
     buffer.get (m);
     consumemessage (m)
  until *false*;

coend

Program 5.1

The monitor which provides the implementation of the bounded buffer problem is as shown in program 4.7, and the two processes which use it are as shown in program 5.1. These two processes (labelled *producer* and *consumer*) make calls to *buffer.put* and *buffer.get* respectively. These calls will therefore be replaced by a "matched pair" of *send* and *receive* calls to pass messages between themselves and a buffer manager process as shown in program 5.2. The details of the buffer manager process have been deferred until later (program 5.3), and we have indulged in a slight abuse of the programming language notation. However, program 5.2 is intended to convey the spirit of the interaction between the two processes and the buffer manager, in that the producer is sending a message to the buffer process which consists of the request that message m be *put* into the buffer. The producer then waits for a message to be returned. It would be very surprising if the value of p returned by the *receive* call were anything other than *buffer*. The m returned in the *receive* call will be a null message, which merely acknowledges that the task has been completed. Similarly, the consumer sends a message to the buffer asking to get a message, and the buffer will eventually oblige and satisfy the *receive* call by returning the next message in the buffer. This message also acts as the acknowledgement of the completion of the operation.

cobegin

buffer: **repeat**
                ...
              until *false*;

producer: **repeat**
                producemessage (*m*);
                send (*buffer*, "*put*", *m*);
                receive (*p*, *m*)
              until *false*;

consumer: **repeat**
                send (*buffer*, "*get* ");
                receive (*p*, *m*);
                consumemessage (*m*)
              until *false*;

coend

Program 5.2

We show the operation of the buffer manager process in program 5.3. This process (like the other two) is in a continuous non-terminating loop, and begins by waiting for a message. When one arrives, it must first determine which function it is to carry out. In this simple case, it will either be a *put* or a *get*.

Consider a request (by the producer) to *put* a message *mess* into the buffer. The buffer manager has first to decide whether there is any space in the buffer to accept the message. If not, then the message is saved in the local variable *savemess*, and the identity of the requesting process is saved in the variable *putprocess*. The purpose of this variable, and of the variable *getprocess*, is to remember the identity of the process whose request has had to be deferred because certain conditions on the data controlled by the manager are not met. In this respect, these variables correspond to the condition variables of the original monitor. The simplifying assumption that there is only one producer and one consumer in the system means that a single variable is sufficient for each condition in this particular case. In general, these variables would have to be capable of remembering a number of processes, and would therefore have to be capable of representing a queue of processes. In the case of a full buffer in the multiple producer

```
buffer:   repeat
             receive (pid, request, mess);
             if request = "put" then
                if n = buffsize then
                begin { buffer is full }
                   savemess := mess;
                   putprocess := pid
                end else
                begin
                   b [p] := mess;
                   send (pid, nullmessage);
                   p := (p + 1) mod buffsize;
                   n := n + 1;
                   if getprocess < > nullprocess then
                   begin
                      mess := b [c];
                      send (getprocess, mess);
                      c := (c + 1) mod buffsize;
                      n := n - 1;
                      getprocess := nullprocess
                   end
                end
             else
             if request = "get" then
                if n = 0 then
                      { buffer is empty }
                   getprocess := pid
                else
                begin
                   send (pid, b [c]);
                   c := (c + 1) mod buffsize;
                   n := n - 1;
                   if putprocess < > nullprocess then
                   begin
                      send (putprocess, nullmessage);
                      b [p] := savemess;
                      p := (p + 1) mod buffsize;
                      n := n + 1;
                      putprocess := nullprocess
                   end
                end
          until false;
```

Program 5.3

situation, the variable *savemess* would also need to be replaced by a queue.

The action of program 5.3 may be described as follows. If space is available in the buffer, then *mess* is placed in the buffer, and the acknowledgement (in the form of a *nullmessage*) returned to the caller. Notice that we have remembered the identity of the calling process, and used this in the reply. It may be, however, that the consumer has already requested a *get* operation. It is therefore necessary for the *put* function to discover whether or not this is the case, and this is done by inspecting the variable *getprocess*. If its value is not *nullprocess*, then the consumer is waiting, and its suspended *get* operation may now be completed, including sending a reply to the consumer process.

If the function requested was a *get*, then the procedure followed is symmetrical, in that the buffer is first tested to see whether there are any messages in it. If not, then the *get* request is held until a message is *put*. Otherwise, the next message is taken out of the buffer and delivered to the calling process using a *send*. Finally, a test is made to see whether there is a pending *put* request, in which case the appropriate action is taken.

It is interesting to compare this buffer manager with the buffer monitor of program 4.7, and to observe how the *signal* and *wait* operations on the condition variable have corresponding program code in the buffer manager. It could be argued that the explicit maintenance of the queues associated with conditions is a drawback to the buffer manager approach, and this is certainly true, but the more active nature of the buffer manager form of the system has a significant advantage over the passive monitor method.

By examining the interaction between either the producer or the consumer and the buffer, it will be seen that following the sending of a message to the buffer, the producer (or consumer) will be delayed until the buffer process replies with a *send* of its own. We can see that, as it is programmed in program 5.3, the buffer performs a *send* at the earliest possible opportunity, i.e. as soon as it has stored (or delivered) the message, and then continues with its own housekeeping tasks, such as updating its own internal pointers and counters. There is no danger in this approach, since the buffer will not begin to process another request until it has completed all its tasks, and has returned to the top of the loop and is ready to receive another message. From this we can see that the "active buffer" approach is able to exploit parallelism to a greater extent than can be achieved using the monitor mechanism, in which all the housekeeping tasks of the buffer have to be performed within the monitor procedures, which preclude the continuation of the calling processes while these tasks are being carried out.

5.8   Exercises

5.1   A message-passing system is described as *synchronous* if the *send* and the *receive* must be executed simultaneously for a message to be passed, and *asynchronous* if a buffering scheme allows the possibility of the *send* being completed some time before the *receive* is executed. In a system in which only the *send* and *receive* operations are available, explain why the distinction between synchronous and asynchronous message-passing is invisible to the communicating processes.

5.2   A server process is frequently coded in the following form:

```
program ServerProcess;
var client : ProcessId;
    mess, rep : Message;
begin
    initialisation;
    repeat
        client := receive (m);
        MainBody;
        { This code is dependent on the content
          of mess and maybe client. }
        send (client, rep) { probably }
    until false
end. { ServerProcess }
```

What would be the implications for the *MainBody* code if
(a)   the server had more than one client?
(b)   in order to provide the requested service, the server had to request service from another server?
(c)   both (a) and (b) were true?

5.3   Why is the mailbox method for inter-process message passing better than the method using direct reference to the target process in the case where a server process wishes to offer a multiplicity of services? How would you get around this difficulty if you did not have this choice?

5.4 Rather than allow processes to create new processes at will, a certain system, whose inter-process communication is based on message passing, has elected to offer a "process management service". This means that any process wishing to establish a new process has to send a request to the process management server, who will reply with information indicating the success or failure of the request, and if successful, the method by which the original requestor may communicate with the new process. What would such a reply contain in the case

(a) where messages are sent directly to a process?

(b) where messages are sent via mailboxes?

5.5 In the problem of the readers and writers (see section 4.4.2), multiple readers were allowed access to the resource, whereas writing to the resource required exclusive access. Design a server to operate within a message-passing environment which exercises the correct control over access to the resource.

5.6 In the solution to exercise 5.5, consider the variations in policy with regard to access to the resource (c.f. exercise 4.11). What policy does your server process implement? How would you modify your server to implement the alternative policy?

5.7 The Sieve of Eratosthanes:

A concurrent version of the Sieve of Eratosthanes method of finding prime numbers is described as follows:

The sequence of numbers 2, 3, 4, 5, etc. is generated by a *generator* process which passes them in the form of messages to a process which will determine for each number whether it is prime or not, and will pass the result back to the generator in the form of another message. In actual fact, this process only checks to see whether each number it receives is divisible by 2 or not. If it is, the number is clearly not prime, and a message to that effect should be returned. If the number is not divisible by 2, then it is passed on to another process to determine whether it is prime. When a reply is received by the "divisible-by-two" process, this answer is forwarded to the generating process.

Thus a chain of processes is created, each member of which is responsible for checking whether a given number n is divisible by a certain prime p. The prime p in some sense represents the identity of the process. If the last process in the chain receives a number which is not a multiple of its "identifying" prime, then a new prime number has been discovered, and (a) this fact must be communicated back along the chain to the generator, and (b) a new process must be created and attached to the end of the chain to detect multiples of this new prime.

Outline the algorithm which each process in the chain (except the generator) must execute in order for this method to work.

5.8   Write a Pascal program to implement a typical process in the chain of processes to detect prime numbers as described in exercise 5.5, given the availability of the following procedures and functions:

send (pr, m)	-	send message m to process pr
$pr := receive$ (m)	-	receive message m from process pr
$pr := newprocess$ (p)	-	create a new process whose identity is pr which is reponsible for detecting multiples of prime p.

You may also assume that each process knows the identity of its predecessor and its successor processes in the chain by the names *pred* and *succ* respectively.

5.9   On the assumption that unconstrained send and receive were used to write the program required by exercise 5.6, what would be the effect on the program, and on the whole system, if the message-passing model used was "send-and-wait-for-reply"?

5.10   Why is it impossible to offer a general service using standard UNIX pipes?

5.11   Is it possible to offer services in UNIX with named pipes? With UNIX messages? With sockets?

5.12   Extend the buffer manager process of program 5.3 to cope with multiple senders and receivers.

6
Languages for Concurrency

Before embarking upon a discussion of the concurrency facilities provided by various programming languages, it is necessary to issue an apology and a warning. The set of languages discussed in this chapter is intended to be a representative selection of languages available at the present time, which between them illustrate a number of different approaches to concurrency. It is hoped that no reader will feel offended at not finding his favourite concurrent language in the discussion. Examples are chosen to demonstrate a variety of treatments of controlled access to shared data, usually in the form of a shared data structure with limited access to the operations on the data structure (i.e. variations on the 'monitor' theme), and also languages supporting some form of message passing or mailbox handling are considered.

It should be clear that beneath each of the mechanisms to be found in any of the languages discussed in this chapter, some lower level code (or hardware) must be supplied to provide, if not the reality, then the illusion of concurrency. Beneath any successful concurrent language there is a system which manages the concurrency, schedules processes onto processors, provides the fundamental operations to implement process creation and deletion, and to provide communication facilities.

When any new language is designed, the designer attempts to correct many of the inadequacies (as he sees them) of one or more existing languages. Many of the languages designed for concurrent programming will include a particular technique to provide the concurrency features, and the designer will be unable to resist the temptation to make other "improvements". For this reason, we observe that a number of different languages will appear to have identical constructs for specifying concurrency and inter-process communication. In the remainder of this chapter we shall try to illustrate various different mechanisms, each of which may appear in a number of different languages. In order to illustrate the use of the various languages, we give an implementation of the same example in each language. In doing so, we attempt to program the example as similarly as possible. This may not necessarily be the best way of coding the example in each language, but will make comparisons of the methods a little easier. The example chosen is our old friend, the bounded buffer.

6.1   Concurrent Pascal

The earliest attempt to introduce concurrency features into a programming language appeared in Concurrent Pascal, a language designed in 1972 by Brinch Hansen. To illustrate the closeness of the perceived relationship between Concurrency and Operating Systems, it is worth noting that Concurrent Pascal was originally intended as a systems programming language, and this fact lay behind some of the design decisions in other areas of the language. This language sought to extend standard Pascal by introducing processes and monitors, while at the same time, some features of the Simula *class* construct were also introduced and some of the features of sequential Pascal which were thought to be unnecessary for system programming were omitted.

Processes and monitors in Concurrent Pascal are declared in the form of *types* and therefore variables of these types may be declared. It is necessary then to cause such variables to become active, and this is achieved using the Concurrent Pascal statement **init**. When an **init** statement is executed, the precise action depends upon whether a process or a monitor is being initialised. In the case of a monitor, the initialisation part of the monitor is executed as a nameless procedure. Processes may then call the procedures and/or functions of the monitor and achieve the normal synchronisation facilities. When a process is the argument of the **init** statement, the code of the process begins to execute asynchronously and independently of all other processes, including the caller of the **init**, i.e. **init** acts like a **fork**. In the case of both monitors and processes, the **init** statement is not responsible for allocating memory in which the monitor or process can store its local variables; this is one consequence of the declaration of the process or monitor.

```
type Producer =
process
    var mess: Message;
    begin
        cycle
            produce (mess);
            buff.send (mess)
        end {cycle}
    end; { Producer }


type Consumer =
process
    var mess: Message;
    begin
        cycle
            buff.receive (mess);
            consume (mess)
        end {cycle}
    end; { Consumer }
```

Program 6.1

Using the bounded buffer example to illustrate the use of Concurrent Pascal, program 6.1 shows the process declarations for the producer and consumer. In these two processes we assume that:

(a)   there is a declaration for the type *Message* appropriate to the application.

and

(b)   there is a monitor called *buff* which implements the bounded buffer.

The *produce* call in the producer and the *consume* call in the consumer are intended to represent the purely local operations concerned with the producing and consuming of each message, respectively. We therefore assume that they require no further elaboration. We note also the use of the construct **cycle** in both processes. Sequential Pascal will allow us to write

repeat ... **until** *false*;

or

while *true* **do** ...;

in order to construct an infinite loop, but in recognition of the fact that in many system programming applications processes frequently require non-terminating loops, Concurrent Pascal allows this to be written as:

cycle ... **end**;

So far the processes are merely specified as types, and as such are only defining the form the process will take. Two further steps are required before these processes actually begin to run. Firstly, an instance of each type of process must be declared, as in the declaration:

var *prod*: *Producer*; *cons*: *Consumer*;

and then they must both be caused to begin their respective executions, and this is achieved using the statement:

init *prod*, *cons*;

In the case of this example, the two processes will run indefinitely, and the question of their termination does not arise. However, it is quite possible for a process declaration to specify code which does terminate, and Concurrent Pascal provides no mechanism for discovering whether a process has terminated. In other words, once a process has been set running asynchronously by a call of **init**, it becomes a free-running program which continues until it reaches the end of its code, at which time it terminates and disappears. As we shall see, this behaviour may be modified by calls to monitor procedures, but if a program so wishes, it can be totally independent of the rest of its environment. It can communicate with other parts of its environment by means of monitors, and if it is necessary for a process to signal its own termination, then a special monitor would have to be written to achieve this.

The principles of the Concurrent Pascal monitor are largely the same as those described in the generalised description of monitors in chapter 4. The monitor provides an implementation of a shared data structure to which mutually exclusive access is allowed by processes calling the monitor procedures. This solves the interference problem, but some additional mechanism is required to provide the inter-process synchronisation which is necessary in some examples such as the bounded buffer problem, namely to exit from the monitor temporarily pending the satisfying of some condition on the monitor data structure. This is available within a Concurrent Pascal monitor by declaring variables of type *queue*. A variable of type *queue* is almost equivalent to the *condition* variable of Hoare's monitor, and the operations which may be performed on a *queue* (apart from the difference in names) are broadly similar to those associated with conditions. These functions may be applied to *queues*:

empty (q)   -   returns true if the queue q has a process in it and false otherwise.

delay (q)   -   the calling process is delayed by being put into queue q and loses its exclusive access to the monitor, thus allowing other processes to enter the monitor.

continue(q)   -   this routine causes an immediate return from the monitor procedure which calls it, and the process in the queue q regains control of the monitor.

Notice that Concurrent Pascal is explicit about the rescheduling of processes, which takes place when either *delay* or *continue* is called. The process ultimately responsible for calling *delay* leaves the monitor immediately and is suspended pending a *continue* operation on the same queue. Similarly, the process calling a *continue* immediately exits the monitor and the "continued" process is immediately re-activated. Observe also that the definition of *continue* refers to *the* process in the queue q. This is because Concurrent Pascal queues are only permitted to hold a maximum of one process, and any attempt to perform a *delay* on an already full queue is regarded as a programming error. A *continue* on an empty queue will still cause the calling process to leave the monitor immediately, but there is clearly no other process to be awoken.

A suitable monitor for implementing the bounded buffer, i.e. to provide the procedures *send* and *receive* as required by the producer and consumer processes of program 6.1, is as shown in program 6.2.

```
type BoundedBuffer =
monitor
    const nmax = ... ; { some suitable value }
    var n: 0..nmax;
        p, c: 0..nmax-1;
        full, empty: queue;
        slots: array [0..nmax-1] of Message;

    procedure entry send (msg: Message);
    begin
      if n = nmax then delay (empty);
      slots [p] := msg;
      p := (p + 1) mod nmax;
      n := n + 1;
      continue (full)
    end; { send }

    procedure entry receive (var msg: Message);
    begin
      if n = 0 then delay (full);
      msg := slots [c];
      c := (c + 1) mod nmax;
      n := n - 1;
      continue (empty)
    end; { receive }

    begin  { initialisation code }
      n := 0; p := 0; c := 0
    end; { monitor BoundedBuffer }
```

Program 6.2

As in the case of processes, this is merely a type definition, and both a declaration and an **init** statement are required to create an instance of the type and to cause the initialisation code to be executed.

Within this monitor, the first identifier is a constant representing the maximum number of messages which the buffer can contain, and would be given a value appropriate to the particular circumstances of the application. After that come the declarations of the various local variables. In particular two variables of type *queue* are introduced, one of which is used to indicate the availability of an empty message slot (*empty*), and the other the presence of at least one message in the buffer (*full*). The word **entry** attached to the procedure declarations for *send* and *receive* is used to indicate that those procedures may be called from outside the monitor. Such a feature is required in order that the monitor may declare procedures which it does not wish the outside world to see or to use. The use of the **entry** attribute is not confined to procedures and functions, but may also be applied to other types of variable as well. However, it would seem to be a valuable principle of good programming that all accesses to the local data of the monitor should really be made using appropriate procedures or functions.

The *queue* type is a powerful construct corresponding closely to the condition type of Hoare's monitor, but as has been noted previously, differs from it in that it may hold at most one process. Clearly, in all its full generality, a variable of type *condition* could have a queue of arbitrary length associated with it. This places a responsibility upon the underlying system to manage a queue of processes, with all the consequent problems of fairness, dispatching, priorities etc. The Concurrent Pascal *queue* avoids such problems, while at the same time placing the responsibility for such considerations on the programmer. It is of course possible for the monitor to contain additional variables in order that real queues of processes may be handled.

In the example given, we assume that there is a single producer and a single consumer process and therefore there can never be more than one process in either queue. If the objective is to provide a general buffering mechanism serving possibly many producers and/or consumers, then the buffer monitor itself would have to make decisions about how many processes may be waiting simultaneously to use the buffer, what to do when that number is exceeded, and how to schedule the restarting of processes following a *continue* operation.

To return to the example, we have already shown the necessary type definitions to set up the two processes and the monitor, so that all that is now required is the main program in which these definitions occur. As before, in addition to the type definitions, we require a declaration of each of the entities and an **init** statement to start them all going, as shown in program 6.3.

```
type   Message = ...;

type   Producer = ...;

type   Consumer = ...;

var    prod: Producer;
       cons: Consumer;
       buff: BoundedBuffer;
begin
       init buff, prod, cons;
end.
```

Program 6.3

The provision of processes and monitors as type definitions within a Concurrent Pascal program provides a high degree of flexibility by allowing several variables to be declared as being of one type. Thus for example, it would be possible to define a pair of buffers provided the structure of and operations upon each were the same. A possible application might be when an input process takes data from the external world, passes it to an intermediate process for manipulation, which in turn passes its results to some output process. We could imagine that the buffer between the input process and the manipulator would have essentially the same structure and characteristics as the buffer between the manipulating process and the output process. Alternatively, we may find examples where multiple instances of a single process type may be useful.

Both processes and monitors may be parameterised, and this clearly is a useful feature, since it provides a channel by which processes can be given some way of identifying themselves, and perhaps more importantly, can be told which instances of variables they are to operate upon. Monitors can in fact be passed as parameters (which is not true of processes), and clearly this enables processes to be told, for instance, which buffer(s) they are to use. A more elegant version of the bounded buffer program might be, therefore, one in which the producer and consumer processes are informed of the buffer through a parameter list, as illustrated in program 6.4.

```
type Message = ...;

type BoundedBuffer = ...; { as before }

type Producer = process (b: BoundedBuffer);
       { body of process as before,
       except for the statement
           buff.send (mess)
       which must be replaced by
           b.send (mess);            }

type Consumer = process (b:BoundedBuffer);
       { slight change to body
       similar to change in body
       of Producer.            }

var buff: BoundedBuffer;
       prod: Producer;
       cons: Consumer;

begin
       init buff, prod (buff), cons (buff)
end.
```

Program 6.4

6.2   Concurrent Euclid

The language Concurrent Euclid was developed at the University of Toronto as an attempt to extend the language Euclid to include concurrency features. Euclid itself had certain design aims, including the requirement that programs in the language would be susceptible to current techniques for program proving. Not surprisingly, some of these features appear in Concurrent Euclid. The differences in the concurrency handling between Concurrent Euclid and Concurrent Pascal are relatively minor, and both create processes essentially as the result of declarations, and both provide inter-process communication using monitors. The main differences lie firstly in the different approach to processes and monitors within the language, and secondly in the semantics of the *condition* within a monitor.

For the purposes of easing the task of proving the correctness of a program, Euclid insists on tight constraints on the program and data structuring features. The basic building block of a Euclid program is the *module*, which provides a class-like facility for the implementation of abstract data types. In Concurrent Euclid, a particular form of the module can be defined, and this is of course the *monitor*, which behaves in the usual way of requiring calls on the monitor procedures to be mutually exclusive. Processes are declared inside modules, and these declarations appear very similar to procedure declarations. Processes begin to run however, as a result of their declarations, and do not require explicit statements to cause them to start their executions. In the case of monitors and of processes, the way in which they are defined precludes their being used as types as in Concurrent Pascal, and in particular it is not possible to declare multiple instances of processes and monitors, neither is it possible to initiate processes at arbitrary points in the code.

6.3   Mesa

The programming language Mesa has been in use for some years internally within the Xerox Corporation, before it was finally published in the open literature. It was designed primarily as a systems programming language, and although it is possible to detect indications of its ancestry, by and large it is a language unlike other languages of its generation. Its primary goals are to provide a very type-safe language, even across the boundaries between separately compiled sections of program. Mesa has the concept of a module, whose function is to provide the ability to partition a program into discrete portions. In particular, Mesa provides an elegant mechanism for defining interfaces, to which both client and server must conform, thus providing a type-checkable connection between separate sections of code. The concurrency features of the language are in keeping with the current ideas at the time the language was designed, and constitute a very flexible set of facilities.

As we saw in chapter 2, new processes in Mesa are created by the use of the FORK operation, which takes a procedure as its argument, and returns a value of type PROCESS as its result. The parent process may resynchronise with the child process thus created by using the JOIN operation, which also provides the opportunity for results to be returned by a child process to its parent. We also saw how this mechanism provided type safety.

Processes in Mesa may require communication between one another beyond the points of creation and termination of the child. This is provided by a variant of the monitor mechanism. Mesa already provides a module structure, which provides all of the desired facilities except for mutual exclusion, and therefore, as we have already seen in Concurrent Euclid, it is simply a matter of allowing the word PROGRAM (the word used in Mesa to mean *module*) to be replaced by the word MONITOR without making any other changes to the structure, and all of the desired properties are available. There are a number of additional features associated with the Mesa MONITOR construct, many of which are beyond the scope of this section (for details refer to the Mesa Language documentation), but there is one detail which we will mention here. Within a MONITOR, it is possible to declare procedures which will have one of the three attributes ENTRY, INTERNAL or EXTERNAL. Procedures designated as being either ENTRY or INTERNAL are simply those procedures which are or are not available to processes outside the monitor. ENTRY procedures claim exclusive access to the data of the monitor, and may use INTERNAL procedures to carry out the desired operation. The attribute EXTERNAL is used to indicate that the procedure may be called from outside the monitor, but unlike an ENTRY procedure, it does not claim exclusive access to the data of the monitor. This feature is useful if there are operations on the monitor data which can safely be performed without exclusive access, but which for reasons of good structuring, should be included in the module comprising the monitor.

Mesa monitors, like Hoare's monitors, require an escape mechanism by which processes can leave the monitor temporarily on discovering that the state of the monitor data is such that the process is unable to continue. This is provided by variables of type CONDITION, as in the following declaration:

    c   :   CONDITION;

Condition variables are used in similar ways to condition variables in monitors in other languages, in that they consist of (possibly empty) queues of processes. The Mesa operations applied to a condition variable c are:

    WAIT c;

and:

    NOTIFY c;   or   BROADCAST c;

The WAIT statement behaves exactly as the corresponding construct in all the other languages we have met, by placing the process calling the WAIT on the queue associated with the condition variable c. The NOTIFY is supposed to perform the same function as a *signal* or *continue* would, but there is an important difference. The Mesa NOTIFY does not force the calling process to leave the monitor immediately, and any process is free to notify a condition at any time and then continue by executing more code within the monitor. There is no obligation on this process to ensure that the monitor invariant is true at the time the NOTIFY is performed. The NOTIFYed process then joins the queue of processes waiting to enter (or maybe re-enter) the monitor until the NOTIFYing process finishes executing the monitor procedure. The consequence of this is that the newly-awoken process will (eventually) re-enter the monitor with the possibility that the NOTIFYing process and/or any other competing process has accessed the monitor data since the NOTIFY, and that the data is once again in the state which prevents the process from continuing. The consequence of this difference is that the process which is awoken by the NOTIFY must recheck the BOOLEAN associated with the condition in order to be sure that continuation is possible. Thus, instead of the construct:

if *BooleanExpression* **then** *wait* (*c*);

such as we might use in Concurrent Euclid, we are required in Mesa to write:

WHILE *BooleanExpression* DO WAIT *c*;

In addition to the NOTIFY, Mesa permits another operation on a condition variable called BROADCAST. This operation allows a process to perform "multiple notifies" to awaken all the processes which may be waiting on the condition. Such a construct could be used to provide an implementation of the *Readers and Writers* problem (Section 4.4.2), where all the waiting readers can be restarted at once using a single call of BROADCAST. The necessity for any notified process to re-examine the Boolean expression associated with a condition variable means that whenever a process wishes to NOTIFY another process, it could also use the BROADCAST, but this may cause unnecessary inefficiencies as a result of waking up a number of processes when only one may be able to continue. As the Mesa Language Manual says:

"It is *always* correct to use a BROADCAST. A NOTIFY may be used if:

It is expected that there will typically be several processes waiting in the condition queue (making it expensive to notify them all with a BROADCAST), and

It is known that the process at the head of the condition variable queue will always be the right one to respond to the situation (making the multiple notification unnecessary)"

To return to our canonical example of the bounded buffer, program 6.5 shows the calling program written in Mesa, showing the producer and consumer processes being FORKed, with the bounded buffer illustrated in program 6.6. Most of the detail relating to the way in which Mesa components are linked together to form a complete

```
ProdCons: PROGRAM =
BEGIN

    MessageType: TYPE = ...;
    prod, cons: PROCESS;

    Producer: PROCEDURE =
    BEGIN
        WHILE true DO
            ProduceMessage [m];
            Buffer.Put [m];
        ENDLOOP;
    END;

    Consumer: PROCEDURE =
    BEGIN
        WHILE true DO
            ProduceMessage [m];
            Buffer.Put [m];
        ENDLOOP;
    END;

    prod ← FORK Producer;
    cons ← FORK Consumer;

END.
```

Program 6.5

program has been omitted, in order not to obscure the main point of this example.

```
BBuffer: MONITOR =
BEGIN

    BuffSize : CARDINAL = ...;
    buff: ARRAY [0..BuffSize) OF ;
    p, c: [0..BuffSize)← 0;
    n: [0..BuffSize]← 0;
    full, empty: CONDITION;

BufGet: PUBLIC ENTRY PROCEDURE
            RETURNS [m : MessageType] =
    BEGIN
        WHILE n = 0 DO WAIT full; ENDLOOP;
        m ← buff[c];
        c ← (c + 1) MOD BuffSize;
        n ← n - 1;
        NOTIFY empty;
        RETURN [m];
    END;

BufPut: PUBLIC ENTRY PROCEDURE
            [m : MessageType] =
    BEGIN
        WHILE n = BuffSize DO WAIT empty; ENDLOOP;
        buff[p] ← m;
        p ← (p + 1) MOD BuffSize;
        n ← n + 1;
        NOTIFY full;
    END;

END.
```

Program 6.6

6.4   Path Pascal

A somewhat different and more flexible approach to the problem of non-interference and control of concurrency is presented by

Campbell et al. in the use of *path expressions* which were discussed in general terms in chapter 4. Path Pascal is a language designed to extend Pascal to provide processes, and controlled access by processes to shared data objects using path expressions. Once again, the language has been modified to provide *encapsulation*, as it is known in Path Pascal, in which the scope of certain variables is restricted to a particular segment or module within the program, and access to those variables is only possible using procedures or functions made available by the module.

The encapsulation construct in Path Pascal is called an *object*, which again looks very similar to a Simula *class*. The data structure is hidden inside the object, and operations are defined by the object to enable processes to manipulate this data. So far, a Path Pascal object looks very similar to a monitor in any of the languages we have examined already. However, whereas in a monitor we enforce total mutual exclusion, i.e. only one process at a time is permitted to be inside the monitor, Path Pascal allows a more flexible specification of the concurrency constraints, and in addition, allows the user to specify some "sequentiality" constraints as well.

As part of the declaration of an object, a path expression may be specified which controls the way in which the operations associated with the object may be used. If we consider again the use of monitors containing condition variables, we see that in many instances, condition variables are used to specify that operations within the monitor may only be executed in certain sequences. For example, the use of the condition *bempty* in the Concurrent Pascal and Concurrent Euclid implementations of the bounded buffer was simply a way of specifying that the *put* procedure must be executed before a *get* (or alternatively, if a *get* is attempted first, it must be delayed until the corresponding *put* has been executed). In fact, we must insist that in order for a *get* to succeed, there must already have been a corresponding *put*. In other words, the total number of *get* operations that can be successfully executed must be less than or equal to the number of *put* operations already completed.

Similarly, since we are assuming that our buffer is bounded, we provided in the Concurrent Pascal and Concurrent Euclid implementations, a condition variable *bfull* , which is used to delay a *put* operation until enough *get* operations have been performed that there is a least one available message position in the buffer.

What these two condition variables are really ensuring is that for each message which is presented to the buffer, a *put* is followed by a *get*, and that only a limited number of *put/get* pairs may be in progress at any one time. Using path expressions, it is possible to ensure that these constraints are satisfied, without the use of condition variables and their corresponding *signals* and *waits* (or *delays* and *continues*).

Suppose we have a bounded buffer of (constant) size N. This means that we must ensure that a *get* operation is not started until its corresponding *put* is complete, but that up to N *puts* which have no corresponding *get* may be executed. The following path expression will provide these constraints:

path N: (*put*; *get*) **end**;

The semi-colon in this expression constrains the use of the operations to ensure that they are only executed in the sequence *put* then *get* (i.e. a *get* may not be started without a *put* having been completed), and furthermore, there can only be N such *put/get* sequences in progress simultaneously.

In the situation in which only one process is acting as producer and only one as consumer, the above solution is perfectly adequate. However, we may wish to consider the more general situation in which there are multiple producers and multiple consumers. Since the path shown above allows up to N simultaneous activations of the path (*put*; *get*), the possibility of up to N simultaneous *put* operations (or *get* operations) is permitted. Clearly this would be undesirable in many implementations, particularly those we have been considering up until now, in that it may lead to destructive interference between processes, and thus we would hope that the path would not only restrict the number of simultaneously active (*put*; *get*) sequences, but also prevent interference as a result of multiple activations of either of the two operations. The path expression required to enforce this additional constraint is of course:

path N: (1: (*put*); 1: (*get*)) **end**;

Since *N* simultaneous activations of the sequence are permitted, but only one concurrent activation of *put* or *get* themselves, we could have one process executing a *put*, one executing a *get*, and up to *N*-2 "waiting at the semi-colon" separating the *put* and *get*. This path would then enforce the desired constraints. If we assume that *N* has the value 10 (say), the full solution, apart from the details of the implementation of the *get* and *put* procedures, is shown as program 6.7.

```
type message = ...;

process producer;
var msg : message;
begin
    repeat
        produce (msg);
        buffer.put (msg)
    until false
end;

process consumer;
var msg : message;
begin
    repeat
        buffer.get (msg);
        consume (msg)
    until false
end;

var buffer = object

    path 10: ( 1: (put); 1: (get)) end;

    procedure get (var m : message); ... ;
    procedure put (m : message); ... ;

end; { object buffer }
```

Program 6.7

In this implementation we have no mechanism for preventing a *put* and a *get* operation from executing at the same time. This in general will not cause any problems, for reasons which will be explained later, but we may notice that in our previous attempts at writing code for the procedures *put* and *get*, both have been required to modify the value of *n*, the number of currently occupied buffer slots, and therefore there is the possibility of interference between these attempts to access/modify this value.

We may also notice, however, that the only use that was made of *n* in the solutions presented previously was to enable the procedures *get* and *put* to decide whether a *wait* or a *signal* on a condition variable was required. In fact, in Path Pascal, the restriction imposed by the path itself is sufficient to ensure that *get*s and *put*s occur in the correct sequence, and that the total number of such sequences is restricted, and therefore it is unnecessary for the number of occupied buffer slots to be referred to explicitly at all. The solution we require to the problem of the buffer object is therefore shown in program 6.8.

This solution to the bounded buffer problem has the merit that not only can we use a path expression to cause the buffer object to behave in a very similar way to a monitor, by controlling the extent of simultaneous access to the monitor, but we have also been able to control the *sequencing* of the operations as well. This means that we no longer require the *signal* and *wait* operations on condition variables as defined in a monitor.

Another observation that can be made about the Path Pascal implementation of the bounded buffer as compared with a conventional monitor implementation is concerned with the possible simultaneous use of *put* and *get*. Clearly, the monitor would enforce total mutual exclusion, and hence *put* and *get* could not be executing simultaneously under any circumstances. In the Path Pascal implementation, the only potential point of interference might occur as a consequence of *put* and *get* attempting to access the same buffer slot simultaneously. But this cannot happen, since we insist that a *get* cannot begin to execute until its corresponding *put* has completed, and hence the *get* for a particular buffer slot is precluded from accessing the same slot as is concurrently the object of a *put* operation (provided we ensure that *p* and *c* are properly initialised).

```
var buffer = object

    path 10: ( 1: (put); 1: (get)) end;
    var p, c : 0..9;
        slots : array 0..9 of message;

    procedure get (var m : message);
    begin
        m := slots [p];
        c := (c + 1) mod 10;
    end;

    procedure put (m : message);
    begin
        slots [p] := m;
        p := (p + 1) mod 10;
    end;

begin { initialisation }
    p := 0; c := 0
end; { object buffer }
```

Program 6.8

We now return to the question of the variable n, the number of occupied buffer slots. As we have observed, the straightforward bounded buffer problem can be solved in Path Pascal without any explicit reference to this value, but we may extend the problem slightly to require that a process may wish to discover how many items there are in the buffer. In other words, the buffer object may be required to offer a function which will return the value of the number of occupied slots. Such a requirement would necessitate the explicit appearance of the variable n. The consequence of this is that both *put* and *get* would need to alter the value of n, and hence a potential point of interference is created.

Fortunately, Path Pascal permits the use of nested objects, and therefore of nested paths. Using this, it is possible to create an object within the buffer object, whose sole function is to control access to the variable n. This object only contains two operations, a function to enable the user to interrogate the value of n, and one integer data item, but its concurrency control is exactly that of a monitor, viz. only one operation may be in progress at any one time. This may be ensured by using the path:

path 1: $(incn, decn, valn)$ **end**;

var *count* = **object**

    path 1: $(incn, decn, valn)$ **end**;
    var n : 0..10;

    procedure *incn*;
    begin
      $n := n + 1$;
    end;

    procedure *decn*;
    begin
      $n := n - 1$;
    end;

    function *valn*: 0..10;
    begin
      $valn := n$
    end;

begin { initialisation }
    $n := 0$
end; { **object** *count* }

Program 6.9(a)

Program 6.9(a) shows the object *count* which includes the path defined above, and program 6.9(b) shows the new version of the object *buffer*, including the extension to the functionality whereby a process may interrogate the number of full buffer slots.

```
var buffer = object

    path 10: ( 1: (put); 1: (get)) end;
    var p, c : 0..9;
        slots : array 0..9 of message;

    var count = object ...

    procedure get (var m : message);
    begin
        m := slots [p];
        c := (c + 1) mod 10;
        count.decn
    end;

    procedure put (m : message);
    begin
        slots [p] := m;
        p := (p + 1) mod 10;
        count.incn
    end;

    function occupancy: 0..10;
    begin
        occupancy := count.valn
    end;

begin { initialisation }
    p := 0; c := 0
end; { object buffer }
```

Program 6.9(b)

6.5   ADA

In all the previous examples in various languages, the implementation of the bounded buffer has employed a passive structure to act as the buffer itself, including the operations needed to manipulate it. Calls are made on the procedures offered by the appropriate program structure whereby the active elements, the producer and the consumer processes, are able to manipulate the buffer in the desired way. The various concurrency structures, monitors, objects containing path expressions, etc. merely specify certain constraints on the way in which these procedures may be used. For the period of time during which the shared data is being manipulated, the called procedure becomes part of the calling process.

The next example we shall give moves away from this idea, and somewhat more towards the message-passing approach. In this case, the buffer itself has an associated "controlling" active element (or process), and the producer(s) and consumer(s) communicate with the "buffer manager" process by means of passing simple messages. In fact, in our next example, the buffer is managed by a separate process (or *task*) and the mechanism for passing data between the producer(s)/consumer(s) and the buffer manager is very similar to a procedure call parameter-passing mechanism.

The language in which this version is written is ADA, which has been designed under sponsorship from the U.S. Department of Defense. Its objectives were to come up with a language which would provide suitable facilities for real-time programming of embedded systems. (Embedded systems are systems in which the computer is only a part of the total system used for online monitoring and control.) Clearly, this implies that some of the programming required will contain an element of "real-time-ness", and also that, in controlling a large and complex system, it will be necessary to have a natural way of expressing the handling of multiple concurrent activities.

An ADA program consists basically of a procedure, within which other procedures may be declared and called. ADA makes a careful distinction between the declaration part of a procedure, known as *elaboration*, in which variables and other constructs are declared, and the executable statements of the procedure. This makes explicit the fact that in declaring new variables, there may well be more involved than merely associating a storage location with a variable name, and possibly assigning it an initial value.

For the record, ADA provides a construct called a *package*, which allows for the grouping together of procedures and data to provide an abstract data type facility, rather like the *module* of

Concurrent Euclid or Mesa, or the *object* of Path Pascal. Packages allow the programmer to structure a system to provide clean, checkable interfaces between the various components, offering all the usual advantages associated with structured programming. Our concern, in respect of concurrency, will not be with packages, although the notion of a process can be included in a package and therefore offered as a service provided by the package.

In fact, ADA uses the word *task* to mean a process, and tasks are declared much as procedures are, in the declarations associated with either an enclosing procedure, or the package in which it is defined. The *elaboration* of the declaration of a task takes place as part of the execution of the enclosing procedure, and therefore tasks begin to execute on entry to the procedure in which they are declared. This procedure is known as the *parent*, and the new task as the *child* task. A procedure is not permitted to terminate until all its child tasks have completed, and a child will only terminate on reaching the end of its code. Thus a measure of synchronisation is provided in respect of the initialisation and termination of tasks. In particular, it can be guaranteed that the number of concurrently active tasks in an ADA program is the same when a procedure returns to its calling environment as it was when that procedure was called, however many additional tasks are started within the procedure.

The rules of scope will of course allow two or more tasks to access variables which are declared in the same or enclosing blocks/procedures, and as a result, it is possible for conflicts to arise when multiple processes attempt to access the same data. In the previous sections of this chapter, the languages discussed have provided a mechanism whereby access to the shared data could be controlled by constraining the extent of simultaneous access to the shared data. ADA has no such construct, but allows a process to offer to synchronise with another process at particular points in their executions. This synchronisation point is called a *rendezvous*.

Using the bounded buffer again as an example, an ADA program to implement the buffer would contain two tasks to act as producer and consumer as before, but instead of making a data structure available to both, and enforcing mutual exclusion (or some other synchronisation constraint) between attempts to access the data structure, we provide a third task to act as buffer manager, and use the rendezvous to provide the necessary synchronisation and data transfer capability. In a certain sense, the buffer ceases to be a shared data structure, and becomes instead private data to the buffer manager task, which then modifies the buffer data structure in response to requests from the "client" tasks. Although the buffer manager is a task in its own right, and is therefore capable of executing independently of the producer and consumer tasks, its function is very much to provide a buffer management service to the other tasks, and will really only be performing useful functions in response to requests from the producer(s) and consumer(s).

We therefore introduce the notion of *active* and *passive* tasks. An active task corresponds more or less with the processes of our previous examples. These are the *client* processes which perform certain functions and which from time to time require a service from another component of the system. In Concurrent Pascal or Concurrent Euclid, for instance, this service is provided by making calls on the procedures of a monitor which perform the required actions as part of the processes which call them. In ADA, these services are provided by another task called a passive task (or *server*). The passive task is so called because it spends most of its time waiting for active tasks to request some kind of service from it.

As far as task creation and termination are concerned, there is no distinction between passive and active tasks, and the differences only manifest themselves when attempts are made to communicate between processes. Communication takes place as a result of two processes synchronising at a particular point in their execution called a *rendezvous*. The difference between an active and a passive task at a rendezvous is that the passive task offers to make a rendezvous with any process which wishes to meet with that task, whereas an active task must request a particular rendezvous with a particular passive task. The passive task contains special constructs within the language called *entries*, whereas the active task makes a call on an entry of a passive task by issuing what is effectively a procedure call. The transfer of information between the two tasks is achieved through what is essentially the parameter list of the procedure call, and the return of results.

It is clear that two tasks wishing to make a rendezvous may not arrive at the point of synchronisation at the same time; in fact it is extremely unlikely that they will. Thus one or other of the processes must wait for the rendezvous to take place. When the two processes do meet, the code of the entry is executed "jointly" by the two processes, after which they part company and go their separate ways. Diagrammatically, we may illustrate the two situations by figures 6.1(a) and (b). In figure 6.1(a), the active task requests a rendezvous

Figure 6.1(a)

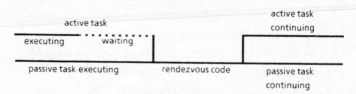

before the passive task is ready to receive the request and therefore has to wait, but in figure 6.1(b), the passive task has to wait pending

Figure 6.1(b)

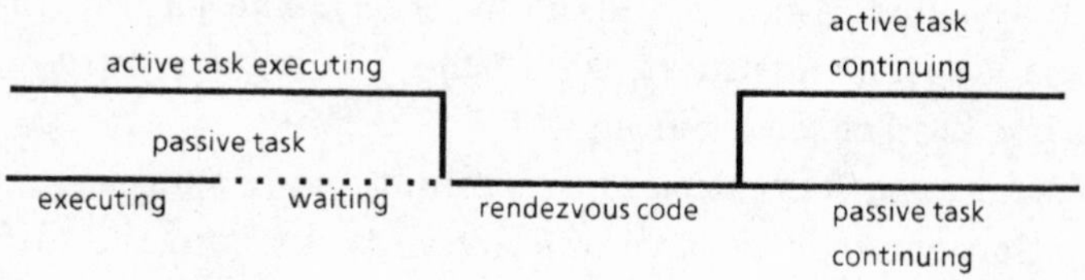

the arrival of a request from the active task.

Returning to the bounded buffer problem, we can immediately see that the monitor or monitor-like structure which implemented the buffer itself in each of our previous solutions to the problem will now be replaced by a passive task in ADA to provide the same effect. The entry points will correspond to the procedures of the monitor, and the initialisation code will be that part of the task's program text which precedes the entry points.

The overall structure of the required ADA program is shown as program 6.10.

In this outline, we observe that there will be three tasks, one of which, *BoundedBuffer*, is offering rendezvous facilities which presumably will be made use of by the other two. The task *BoundedBuffer* will therefore be a passive task, and the assumption is

MessageSystem:
  declare
    MessType = ...

    task *Producer*;
    task *Consumer*;

    task *BoundedBuffer* **is**
      entry *Get* (*mess*: **out** *MessType*);
      entry *Put* (*mess*: **in** *MessType*);
    end *BoundedBuffer*;

    -- task bodies for the tasks *Producer*, *Consumer*
    -- and *BoundedBuffer* may either be declared
    -- here, or separately for later linking.
  begin
    -- null body, since all the work is done by the tasks
  end *MessageSystem*;

Program 6.10

that both *Producer* and *Consumer* will be active tasks. When *MessageSystem* is called, the elaboration of all its declarations takes place, including the initiation of the three tasks, and the (null) body begins to execute. This body, despite the fact that it has nothing to do, cannot terminate until each of its children has terminated. (In fact, in this case, we shall see that the children are all designed to run indefinitely, and therefore none of the children nor the parent *MessageSystem* will terminate.)

As noted in the comment in the program above, ADA will permit the bodies of the various tasks to be specified either within the main program, or else may be specified and compiled separately, and linked with the main program at a later time. The task bodies for the *Producer* and *Consumer* tasks are as might be expected, and appear as program 6.11.

As before, we shall leave the precise action of the procedures *ProduceMessage* and *ConsumeMessage* unspecified. These merely indicate that the tasks have some local processing to do concerned with

```
task body Producer is
    pmess: MessType;
    begin
      loop
        ProduceMessage (pmess);
        BoundedBuffer.Put (pmess);
      end loop;
    end Producer;

task body Consumer is
    cmess: MessType;
    begin
      loop
        BoundedBuffer.Get (cmess);
        ConsumeMessage (cmess);
      end loop;
    end Producer;
```

Program 6.11

the initial source of the message data, and its ultimate destination. The statements in these two processes concerned with using the bounded buffer appear very similar to the calls on monitor procedures as specified in the previous examples. In ADA, however, they are interpreted as requests to rendezvous with the passive task *BoundedBuffer* at one of its entry points.

We now examine the task *BoundedBuffer* in more detail to show how the entry points are specified, and the action taken by the passive task before, during and after the rendezvous takes place. A passive task begins to execute as a result of its elaboration, just as an active task does. This provides the opportunity for the passive task to perform such initialisation statements as may be required. It then reaches an entry point, specified by an **accept** statement, and waits there for the rendezvous to take place. It may be that an active process has already reached its call to the entry point, in which case the passive task will not be delayed. During the rendezvous statements, the two processes proceed together, and when the end of the rendezvous is reached, the two tasks again continue along their separate paths, the passive task executing its final statements. The general layout of a passive task is shown in program 6.12.

```
task body TaskName is
    -- declarations of local identifiers
    begin
        -- initialisation statements
        accept RendezVousName (parameters) do
            -- rendezvous statements
        end RendezVousName;
        -- final statements
    end TaskName;
```

Program 6.12

This describes the structure of the passive task in only the barest outline, and is clearly insufficient for the bounded buffer example. Firstly, we already know that the producer and consumer tasks are expecting the buffer to be continuously available, and therefore the *BoundedBuffer* task must include an infinite loop. Secondly, the buffer must offer two rendezvous points called *Get* and *Put* and therefore there will have to be two **accept** statements. Furthermore, there is no way of telling which order the requests for a rendezvous will occur, and thus a mechanism must be provided whereby the task can select which rendezvous to accept depending on which entry point is being called. ADA provides a **select** statement precisely for this purpose. Thirdly, the facility corresponding to the monitor's condition variable, which prevents the rendezvous from taking place unless a particular condition on the buffer data structure is true must be included in the mechanism. This is achieved by allowing a Dijkstra-style *guard* to be associated with each entry point, designated by a **when** clause preceding the **accept**. The combination of the **select** statement and the guarded **accept** statement gives the appearance of a set of parallel statements each of which may be controlled by a Boolean guard and an input guard.

The full version of the *BoundedBuffer* task is now given as program 6.13.

Now we see that the action of this task, following the initialisation statements, is contained within a **loop** statement, which

```
task body BoundedBuffer is
    maxslots: constant integer := 32;
    buff        : array (1..maxslots) of MessType;
    p, c        : integer range 1.. maxslots;
    nslots      : integer range 0..maxslots;
begin
    p := 1; c := 1; nslots := 0;
    loop
      select
        when nslots > 0 = >
        accept Get (mess : out MessType) do
            mess := buff (c);
        end Get;
        c := c mod maxslots + 1;
        nslots := nslots - 1;
      or
        when nslots < maxslots = >
        accept Put (mess : in MessType) do
            buff (p):= mess ;
        end Put;
        p := p mod maxslots + 1;
        nslots := nslots + 1;
      or
        terminate;
      end select;
    end loop;
end BoundedBuffer;
```

Program 6.13

means it will execute indefinitely. The two possible entry points, specified by the **accept** statements, are included within a

select ... or... or ... end select

construction, which enables an entry point to be a candidate for execution whenever there is a call on that entry point by an active process, and the **when** *Boolean_expression* = > construction acts as a guard on the **accept** statement. In this particular example, only the entry points *Get* and *Put* are ever called by the active processes, but ADA does provide a mechanism whereby a passive task can recognise and take remedial action in the event of an unexpected rendezvous being requested. This is not the right place to deal with the intricacies of ADA exception handling, but the use of the **terminate** statement allows a passive task to "escape" if it is called in an unscheduled manner.

As was pointed out in section 5.7, there is one further observation which can be made concerning solutions to concurrency problems by means of additional processes as opposed to inactive structures such as monitors. In an environment in which shared data is protected by some passive structure, all of the activity involving the shared data has to be carried out as part of the process calling the monitor procedure. If we examine the problem closely, however, we observe that some of the operations within the procedure are purely housekeeping on the part of the shared data structure, and apart from the need to keep the data structure consistent, is of no concern to the calling process. In the case of a system or language in which the management of the data structure is handled by an active element (an ADA task is an active element, despite the fact that *BoundedBuffer* is called a *passive* task), the completion of the actual rendezvous allows the client (active) task to continue with its own work, and leave the housekeeping to be done by the buffer management task at the same time. In this case, the producer and consumer tasks are not concerned with the internal details of the incrementation of p or c, nor of the incrementation or decrementation of *nslots*. All they care about is depositing a message in the buffer, or taking one out.

6.6   Pascal-m

ADA gives us our first example of a language in which constructs other than shared memory and shared memory access controls are provided for communication between concurrent processes and tasks. In ADA, however, it is possible to access variables within parallel tasks which have been declared in an enclosing scope. In this sense, ADA is a language which supports the shared memory model, but it offers no facilities for protecting shared variables against simultaneous access, and thus we must conclude that ADA's preferred method for inter-task communication is that provided by the rendezvous mechanism, and hence that inter-task communication in ADA is essentially message-based.

The language Pascal-m is very clearly intended to provide concurrent processes which communicate via message passing. In fact, it is so arranged that processes are unable to access shared variables, and communication takes place through special message channels called *mailboxes*. Objects of type **mailbox** may be created outside the scope of a set of processes, and then used by those processes to pass information amongst themselves. Only two operations are permitted on mailboxes, *send* and *receive*, which have the expected meanings. When a mailbox is defined, a type is associated with the mailbox, and only messages of that type may be passed using that mailbox.

The fundamental construct of a Pascal-m program is the *module*, and indeed, a complete program is itself an anonymous module. Within a module, it is possible to define constants and types, to declare other modules and processes, and also to create objects called mailboxes. Notice, however, that no variable declarations may appear within a module at this level. This is deliberate, and it effectively prevents processes from sharing variables. Inter-process communication is achieved using the mailbox construct, as we shall see later. Processes, on the other hand, are capable of creating variables, but these are purely local to the process, and are not available outside the process, and in particular to other processes.

Module and process declarations on their own do not create modules and processes. The declarations are essentially similar to type definitions, as in Concurrent Pascal, in that they merely describe the structure and actions of the module or process. The actual creation of the entity is achieved via **instance** statements, and these are the only kind of statements which may appear in the body of a module. This facility of course gives the opportunity of creating multiple identical processes, or indeed if one wished, multiple identical modules.

Since the outermost level of the program is itself a module, its definition cannot therefore be included in an enclosing module which also includes an instantiation of the module. The program must therefore consist of a module definition and instantiation at the same time, and the facility for providing this capacity is available more generally in the **module instance** statement. This allows for the definition and instantiation of a module in one single construct, and hence may be used to create whole programs. While the ability to define a single process and then create several instances of it offers a great deal of useful flexibility, it is often the case that a single instance of a process is sufficient, in which case a **process instance** construct will define and instantiate a process at the same time.

As we mentioned earlier, no communication between processes may take place using shared variables, since the syntax of the language prevents the declaration of variables in positions where more than one process can access them. Processes may however communicate using mailboxes, whose declarations may appear at the outermost level within a module definition. Thus two processes may name the same mailbox, and thereby communicate with each other. Mailboxes are essentially message buffers with space for a single message. In addition, communication through a mailbox is synchronous, (i.e. the communicating processes must meet at the moment of passing the message), and the type of message which may be passed via the mailbox is specified at the time of the declaration of the mailbox.

The only operations which are permitted using mailboxes are:

send *a* **to** *mbox*

and:

receive *b* **from** *mbox*

If we assume that these two statements are in different processes, say *P1* and *P2* respectively, then program 6.14 shows the outline of the Pascal-m program required, and in particular the definitions of the entities necessary for this exchange of data to occur. For the time being, we may disregard the **import** statements, suffice it to note that they are necessary to make the mailbox *mbox* accessible to the bodies of the processes *P1* and *P2*.

The first remark to be made concerns the definition of the mailbox itself. The construct

```
module instance Main;
    ...
    type T = ...; { whatever }
    type MOT = mailbox of T;
    mailbox mbox : MOT;
    ...
    process instance P1;
        import mbox : MOT;
    var a : T;
    begin
        ...
        send a to mbox;
        ...
    end; { process instance P1 }

    process instance P2;
        import mbox : MOT;
    var b : T;
    begin
        ...
        receive b from mbox;
        ...
    end; { process instance P2 }

    ...
    end; { module instance Main }
```

Program 6.14

mailbox *mbox* : **mailbox of** *T*;

(except that in program 6.14 we defined *MOT* to be a synonym for
mailbox of *T*, and used that instead) causes a mailbox to be created
and the name *mbox* to be defined as the identifying value (or

identification) for this newly created mailbox. It also specifies that only messages of type T may be passed through the mailbox. It is important to distinguish between the construct above and

var mbx : **mailbox of** T;

This latter construct does not create a mailbox, but merely creates a variable capable of storing values of type "**mailbox of** T". Thus the statement

$mbx := mbox$;

is perfectly acceptable, and thereafter mbx can be used in place of $mbox$, as in

send a **to** mbx;

Note however that the declaration alone creates an uninitialised variable, and any attempt to refer to the variable, for example in a **send** statement, prior to its being given a value would have disastrous consequences. The full significance of mailbox variables will become apparent later.

The synchronous nature of the communication through mailboxes means that, referring again to program 6.13, either process *P1* will wait at the **send** statement, or *P2* will wait at the **receive**, until the other process reaches its corresponding statement. When this happens, the value of the variable a (which could in general be an expression) will be passed through the mailbox $mbox$, and assigned to the variable b. Only then are the two processes permitted to continue with their independent computations.

Now let us consider how we might implement the bounded buffer program using Pascal-m. Clearly, because mailboxes can only hold one message at a time, and because mailbox communication is synchronous, it is not possible to use the mailbox mechanism as it is. We need to create some space (i.e. a data structure) which can be used to store the messages which have been sent to the buffer and which have not yet been received, and to handle the necessary housekeeping.

Perhaps our first attempt might look something like program 6.15. We observe that, as in the example using ADA, we have a producer and a consumer process looking very similar to the processes we have been using in every case, and we also have a buffer manager process, the details of which are shown in program 6.16.

Unfortunately, this is about as useful as solution 4 of the critical section problem (program 3.8). What in fact will happen is that *BufferManager* will wait until *Producer* is ready to communicate, and *Consumer* will also be waiting to communicate through *getbox*. When *Producer* is ready, *BufferManager* will take the message from *putbox* and put it into *slots*[p], increment p and then attempt to synchronise with *Consumer* at the communication through *getbox*. At this point, the message to be passed to *Consumer* is taken from *slots*[c], which happens to be the same slot as was used in the immediately previous communication with *Producer*. In other words, only one message will ever be in the buffer, and *Producer* and *Consumer* will be completely synchronised with each other.

This problem arises because the buffer manager process tries to take an active rôle in its dealings with *Consumer*. However, since it is a sequential process, and mailbox communication is synchronous, it is not possible for *BufferManager* to offer a **send** on *getbox* and simultaneously offer a **receive** on *putbox*. This simultaneous action is not a requirement, but it will suffice to recognise that there will be some non-determinism in the pattern of requests to put and get messages. In a very similar way to that provided by ADA, Pascal-m resolves the non-determinism by using a **select** statement. Of course, the bounded buffer program still requires the consumer to wait if the buffer is empty and the producer to wait if the buffer is full, and so the **select** mechanism includes the same facility as ADA for guarding the various non-deterministic communications which may be attempted. The **select** statement therefore consists of

```
module instance MessageSystem;

type   T = ...;
       MOT = mailbox of T;
mailbox   putbox,
          getbox : MOT;

     process instance Producer;
       import putbox : MOT;
     var pmess : T;
     begin
       repeat
         ProduceMessage (pmess);
         send pmess to putbox;
       until false
     end; { process instance Producer }

     process instance Consumer;
       import getbox : MOT;
     var cmess : T;
     begin
       repeat
         receive cmess from getbox;
         ConsumeMessage (cmess);
       until false
     end; { process instance Consumer }

     process instance BufferManager;
       import getbox, putbox : MOT;
       ...

end; { module instance MessageSystem }
```

Program 6.15

```
select
    if Guard₁ then MessageOffer₁ :
        Statement₁;
    if Guard₂ then MessageOffer₂ :
        Statement₂;
    ...
    if Guardₙ then MessageOfferₙ :
        Statementₙ
end; { select }
```

In this construct, $Guard_1,...,Guard_n$ represent Boolean expressions, and each of $MessageOffer_1,...,MessageOffer_n$ is either a **send** or a **receive** statement on a mailbox. The guard part is optional, its absence being equivalent to a true guard. The operation of the **select** statement is to wait until one of the message offer parts receives a matching offer (i.e. a **receive** or **send** on the same mailbox), and the corresponding guard is true (or *enabled*). At this point the communication takes place and the **select** statement terminates. If it should happen that none of the guards are enabled (almost certainly

```
process instance BufferManager;
    import getbox, putbox : MOT;
const BufSize = 32;
    BufTop = 31;
var p, c : 0.. BufTop;
    slots : array [0..BufTop] of T;
begin
    p := 0; c := 0;
    repeat
        receive slots [p] from putbox;
        p := (p + 1) mod BufSize;
        send slots [c] to getbox;
        c := (c + 1) mod BufSize
    until false
end; { process instance BufferManager }
```

Program 6.16

representing a meaningless situation), then the process is aborted. The behaviour of the select statement reflects the alternative version of the guarded command construct introduced in chapter 2 (section 2.3.2).

Pascal-m also has a statement corresponding to the repetitive guarded command structure called **repselect**. As with repetitive guarded commands, **repselect** continuously loops until none of the guards is enabled, at which point it terminates.

Using these notions, we may now show (in program 6.17) a

```
process instance BufferManager;
    import getbox, putbox : MOT;
const BufSize = 32;
    BufTop = 31;
var p, c : 0.. BufTop;
    n : 0.. BufSize;
    slots : array [0..BufTop] of T;
begin
    p := 0; c := 0; n := 0;
    repselect
    if n < BufSize then receive slots [p] from putbox :
    begin
        p := (p + 1) mod BufSize;
        n := n + 1
    end;
    if n > 0 then send slots [c] to getbox :
    begin
        c := (c + 1) mod BufSize;
        n := n - 1
    end
    end { repselect }
end; { process instance BufferManager }
```

Program 6.17

more useful version of the buffer manager process.

In this example, we have declared our three processes and instantiated them at the same time, i.e. we have used **process instance** to introduce each one. In order to make the communication channels available, we have also had to import the mailboxes into the processes which need to have access to them. If, on the other hand, we had introduced our processes using **process** (as opposed to **process instance**), we would then need to have provided separate **instance** statements actually to create the processes and start their execution. Using this method for declaring and starting processes allows the possibility of creating multiple identical processes, and in this particular example, multiple producers, consumers and buffer managers could be created.

When processes (and modules if required) are introduced in this way, it is permissible to specify a formal parameter list at the declaration stage, and to supply actual parameters at instantiation. Parameters may either be constants, or more commonly, mailboxes which the particular instance of the process will use for communication. Thus our message system might appear as in programs 6.18 and 6.19.

If we now wished our system to be extended to contain another producer/consumer pair, communicating through another bounded buffer possibly of a different size, we should merely have to declare two more mailboxes:

var *getbox1, putbox1*;

and instantiate another set of processes:

instance *p1* = *Producer* (*putbox1*);
         b1 = *BufferManager* (*putbox1, getbox1, 16*);
         c1 = *Consumer* (*getbox1*);

We conclude our discussion of Pascal-m by elaborating upon the ability in Pascal-m to declare variables of type *mailbox*. It will be recalled that the declaration of a mailbox variable does not create a mailbox (which is achieved by the use of the **mailbox** definition), but merely a variable capable of taking a mailbox value. The idea of being able to transfer values of type mailbox around is particularly useful when it is also realised that such values may be passed as part of messages. Two examples will illustrate ways in which this feature may be used.

module instance *MessageSystem;*

type *T* = ...;
    MOT = **mailbox of** *T*;
mailbox *putbox,*
    getbox : *MOT;*

  process *Producer* (*in* : *MOT*);
  var *pmess* : *T*;
  begin
    repeat
      ProduceMessage (*pmess*);
      send *pmess* **to** *in*
    until *false*
  end; { **process** *Producer* }

  process *Consumer* (*out* : *MOT*);
  var *cmess* : *T*;
  begin
    repeat
      receive *cmess* **from** *out*;
      ConsumeMessage (*cmess*)
    until *false*
  end; { **process** *Consumer* }

  process *BufferManager* (*in, out* : *MOT*; *size* : *integer*);
    ...

  instance *p* = *Producer* (*putbox*);
    b = *BufferManager* (*putbox, getbox*, 32);
    c = *Consumer* (*getbox*);

end; { **module instance** *MessageSystem* }

Program 6.18

```
process BufferManager (in, out : MOT; size : integer);
var p, c : 1.. size;
    n : 0.. size;
    slots : array [1..size] of T;
begin
    p := 1; c := 1; n := 0;
    repselect
        if n < size then receive slots [p] from in :
        begin
            p := p mod size + 1;
            n := n + 1
        end;
        if n > 0 then send slots [c] to out :
        begin
            c := c mod size + 1;
            n := n - 1
        end
    end { repselect }
end; { process instance BufferManager }
```

Program 6.19

The first example concerns the client/server model of inter-process communication which was discussed in section 5.2. Any process which is prepared to offer service to other processes must inform all potential users of that service how access to the process may be gained. In section 5.3, this was described in terms of the identity of the server process being made generally available. In Pascal-m, the same effect may be obtained by broadcasting the identity of a mailbox by which the server may be contacted. In fact, by programming the server using a **select** statement, a different mailbox could be used for each separate service offered by the server.

In our previous discussion of the client/server model, we assumed that the identity of the client process would be made known to the server using the request message, and hence the server would discover the destination of the reply message. In Pascal-m however, process names, if they exist at all, are not used for this purpose, inter-process communication being achieved by naming mailboxes rather than processes. One way in which clients may be able to receive replies from a server would be through another known mailbox. That is, the server must broadcast not only the identity of the mailbox (or mailboxes) through which service requests may be submitted, but also the identity of the mailbox(es) by which the client must receive the reply.

This situation is far from satisfactory, since it is perfectly possible for another process, either accidentally or maliciously, to attempt to receive a message on the (well-known) reply mailbox, thus preventing the true client from obtaining his response. This in itself is highly undesirable, but if we further postulate that the service is perhaps providing sensitive information, as, for instance, an authentication service returning confidential authentication data, the ability of other processes to "tap" replies could seriously compromise the integrity of the whole system.

So we need to look for an alternative method for servers to reply to their clients, and we may make use of Pascal-m's ability to pass mailbox values in messages to provide such a mechanism. The server is still required to publish the identity of the mailbox(es) by which service requests are sent, but now we assume that a mailbox value is sent with the request, and this is interpreted as the route by which the reply is to be returned to the client. To demonstrate this, we give a small example of a server which offers an arithmetic service. We assume that this process takes two integers and, depending on the mailbox through which the request arrives, returns the sum, difference or product of the two. The result will of course be an integer. Program 6.20 shows the module using a well-known mailbox to return the result.

As indicated, the fact that *TypicalClient* calls **receive** immediately following the **send** cannot guarantee that the results are returned correctly, since any process within the system can have access to the *results* mailbox, and may have already attempted a **receive** naming this mailbox. This will succeed ahead of the **receive** call made by *TypicalClient*.

A much safer method is illustrated in program 6.21(a) and (b). In this case we wish to make our reply mailbox private to the *TypicalClient* process. Unfortunately, mailbox definitions are not permitted in a process declaration, so it is necessary for the typical

```
module instance Main;

type  operands  =   record
                op1, op2 : integer
            end;
mailbox
    add, subtract, mult : mailbox of operands;
    results : mailbox of integer;

    process instance ArithOps;
        import add, subtract, mult, results;
        var inops : operands;
        begin
            repselect
                receive inops from add :
                    send inops.op1 + inops.op2 to results;
                receive inops from subtract :
                    send inops.op1 - inops.op2 to results;
                receive inops from mult :
                    send inops.op1 * inops.op2 to results
            end { repselect }
        end; { process instance ArithOps }

    process instance TypicalClient;
        import subtract, results;
        var ops : operands;
            res : integer;
        begin
            ops.op1 := 28; ops.op2 := 15;
            send ops to subtract;
            receive res from results
        end; { process instance TypicalClient }

end; { module instance Main }
```

Program 6.20

```
module instance Main;

type operands  =     record
                     op1, op2 : integer;
                     replybox : mailbox of integer
               end;
     operbox   =     mailbox of operands;

module instance ArithOps;
    export add, subtract, mult : operbox;

    mailbox
        add, subtract, mult : operbox;

    process instance PerformOps;
        import add, subtract, mult;
    var inops : operands;
    begin
        repselect
            receive inops from add :
                send inops.op1 + inops.op2 to inops.replybox;
            receive inops from subtract :
                send inops.op1 - inops.op2 to inops.replybox;
            receive inops from mult :
                send inops.op1 * inops.op2 to inops.replybox
        end { repselect }
    end; { process instance PerformOps }

end; { module instance ArithOps }

module instance TypicalClient;
        ... { see program 6.21(b) }

end; { module instance Main }
```

Program 6.21(a)

```
module instance TypicalClient;
    import add, subtract, mult : operbox;

mailbox
    reply : mailbox of integer;

process instance DoSub;
    import subtract;
var ops : operands;
    res : integer;
begin
    ops.op1 := 28; ops.op2 := 15;
    ops.replybox := reply;
    send ops to subtract;
    receive res from reply { or ops.replybox }
end; { process instance DoSub }

end; { module instance TypicalClient }
```

Program 6.21(b)

client process to be written as a module, with a process inside it to do the work, and the private mailbox may then be defined within the module. For consistency and good style, we have also encapsulated the *ArithOps* server as a module, and we notice that this module has to **export** the mailboxes which clients are permitted to use.

In this way we are able to ensure that only the process *DoSub* in the *TypicalClient* module (and any other process which may be defined in it) is capable of performing a receive on the mailbox reply, since no other process knows of its existence. We assume that the server can be trusted not to make a copy of the identity of this mailbox with a view to broadcasting it to other processes!

The other example of the use of a mailbox to pass mailbox values is that of a name server. When we discussed the use of name servers in section 5.4, we indicated the disadvantages of every process needing to know the identities of every server it might ever wish to contact. The same comment may be made about mailboxes, and the necessity of each potential client process knowing the names of all the

```
module instance Main;

type  FSreply =  ...;
      FSrequest =    record
                  ...;
              fsreplybox : mailbox of FSreply
              end;
      NSreply =    mailbox of FSrequest;
      NSrequest =    record
                  fsname : Name;
                  nsreplybox : mailbox of NSreply
                  end;
      NSinbox=    mailbox of NSrequest;

module instance NameServer;
    export nsrequestbox : NSinbox;

    mailbox
    nsrequestbox : NSinbox;

    process instance PerformLookUp;
      import nsrequestbox : NSinbox;
    var inreq : NSrequest;
      fsbox : NSreply;
    begin
      repeat
        receive inreq from nsrequestbox;
        fsbox := LookUp (inreq.fsname);
        send fsbox to inreq.nsreplybox
      until false
    end; { process instance PerformLookUp }

end; { module instance NameServer }

module instance FileServiceClient;
      ... { see program 6.22(b) }

end; { module instance Main }
```

Program 6.22(a)

```
module instance FileServiceClient;
    import nsrequestbox : NSinbox;

mailbox
    nsanswerbox : mailbox of NSreply;
    fsanswerbox : mailbox of FSreply;

process instance DoFSrequest;
    import nsrequestbox : NSinbox;
var nsask : NSrequest;
    fsreqbox : NSreply;
    fsask : FSrequest;
    fres : FSreply;
begin
    nsask.fsname := 'MyFileService';
    nsask.nsreplybox := nsanswerbox;
    send nsask to nsrequestbox;
    receive fsreqbox from nsanswerbox;
    { set up file service request in fsask }
    fsask.fsreplybox := fsanswerbox
    send fsask to fsreqbox;
    receive fres from fsanswer
end; { process instance DoFSrequest }

end; { module instance FileServiceClient }
```

Program 6.22(b)

mailboxes which it must use to contact any service it might require.

The name server may be used in the same way as before, except that it now responds to requests by passing mailbox values rather than process identities. Thus, in program 6.22(a) and (b), we see a method for contacting a file service, for instance, given that the client knows the name of the file service, and the means (i.e. the mailbox) whereby the name service can be accessed.

6.7   OCCAM

The OCCAM language, invented by Inmos Ltd., takes a somewhat different approach to concurrency than any of those considered up till now, although some similarities with the previous constructs may be identifiable. The language was developed as the natural way in which to express the behaviour of a specific device known as the *transputer*, but the language has much more applicability than just to this device. However, in considering programs written in OCCAM, it is useful to regard the constructs of the language as representing hardware functions, and the communication between language constructs as modelling the flow of information between hardware components.

The primitives of the language consist of *processes* of three types: input, output and assignment. Input/output is performed over *channels*, and it is necessary for an input statement or process and an output process specifying the same channel to be simultaneously active for the input/output to take place. The assignment process is used for assigning the value of an expression to a variable.

OCCAM processes are not unlike processes as we have already discussed them, but in general they will be of much finer granularity. In fact, the three types of process are represented in OCCAM by the notation:

input	-	$c?v$	- which specifies that the variable v is to receive the value being delivered on channel c.
output	-	$c!e$	- which specifies that the value of the expression e is to be output on channel c.
assignment	-	$v := e$	- in common with most assignments, this specifies that the value of the expression e is to be assigned to the variable v.

Programs are built by combining together these primitive processes using *constructors*. OCCAM provides five constructors, as follows:

SEQ   -   the processes under the control of this constructor are carried out in strict sequence, each one starting only when its predecessor has completed.

PAR   -   all the processes begin to execute concurrently. A **PAR** construct will only terminate when all its component processes have terminated.

IF   -   allows (or denies) execution of a process according to the value of some Boolean expression.

WHILE   -   iterates a set of processes until a Boolean expression becomes *false*.

ALT   -   uses the notion of Boolean guards and input guards to select one of a set of processes for execution.

In order to keep some consistency with earlier sections of this chapter, the solution to the bounded buffer problem will be programmed in a way similar to that used before. In fact, it transpires that OCCAM, based as it is on notions associated with hardware components, has a more natural way of solving the same problem, and this program will also be presented later on in this section.

The primitives of OCCAM lend themselves to the message-based approach to concurrency, but as we discussed in Chapter 5, the analogy between message-based and procedure-based concurrency allows us to translate the procedure-based version of the bounded buffer problem from Concurrent Euclid (say) into OCCAM without any difficulty.

The overall structure of the OCCAM program is shown as program 6.23.

Before we continue with the discussion of the problem and its solution, some further explanation of the syntax of OCCAM is required. Firstly, notice that the scope of each of the constructors is determined by the level of indentation of each process which follows it. Thus, there are three processes controlled by the initial **PAR** constructor, namely the three **WHILE** processes preceded by the comments Producer code, Consumer code and Buffer code. Also, within the producer and the

PAR
-- Comments are introduced by two dashes.

  -- Producer code
  WHILE *true*
  VAR *m*:
    SEQ
      -- produce message *m*
      inch!*m*

  -- Consumer code
  WHILE *true*
  VAR *m*:
    SEQ
      outch?*m*
      -- consume message *m*

  -- Buffer code
  WHILE *true*
    -- See later

Program 6.23

consumer, a local variable *m* has been declared using the **VAR** keyword. No type has been given to the variable, and for the time being we shall assume that there are no types in OCCAM. Finally, we have assumed in writing the producer and consumer code that the buffer can accept messages on the channel *inch*, and will deliver messages on the channel *outch*.

We now need to consider the implementation for the buffer itself. The variables which we require are essentially the same as those required in the previous versions, and they have the same meanings. Program 6.24 shows an initial attempt.

We will first explain the action of this program and then examine it in detail to determine whether or not it satisfactorily solves the problem. The first step is to declare three local variables *n*, *p* and *c*, and a local array *b*. These have precisely the same meanings as they have done in the previous examples. Notice, however, that when we

```
DEF nmax = ...          -- Some appropriate value
VAR p, c, n:
VAR b[n]:
  SEQ
    p := 0
    c := 0
    n := 0
    WHILE true
      ALT
        (n < nmax) & inch?b[p] = >
          PAR
            n := n + 1
            SEQ
              p := p + 1
              p := p \ nmax
        (n > 0) & SKIP = >
          PAR
            n := n - 1
            SEQ
              outch!b[c]
              c := c + 1
              c := c \ nmax
```

Program 6.24

declare the array b, we specify the number n of elements it should have, but they are indexed by the numbers $0..n\text{-}1$, rather than by $1..n$. In order to ensure that these variables are properly initialised before the main part of the buffer handling is entered, we specify that these initialisation statements are performed sequentially before the main **WHILE** clause. In fact, there is no reason why the three initialisation statements should occur in any particular order, and indeed we could allow them all to occur in parallel. However, they must all have been completed before the facilities of the buffer are made available to the producer and consumer processes.

Within the **WHILE** clause, the process is prepared to take one of two actions depending upon the prevailing conditions. Having embarked upon one of the actions (and the one it chooses is purely arbitrary, although in practice there will be some underlying queuing arrangement which is assumed to be fair), that action will be completed before the loop is re-executed, and another choice is made. The two actions are "guarded" by the two conditions, the first of which is the combination of a Boolean guard and an input guard, and the second of which is just a Boolean guard. To select the first alternative, the buffer must first of all have an available slot (indicated by $n < nmax$), and also there must be a process offering a value to be stored (indicated by $inch?b[p]$ being satisfied). For the second alternative to be selected, all that is required is for there to be at least one value stored in the buffer (denoted by $n > 0$). An OCCAM guard has an optional Boolean guard and a mandatory input guard. However, in this case the "input" guard needs to be empty, and the **& SKIP** construct provides this facility.

The code which appears within the two arms of the **ALT** clause use a combination of **SEQ** and **PAR** constructors to provide the maximum degree of concurrency. The updating of the variable n in each case can occur in parallel with the other actions, but the incrementation of p or c followed by the modulo operation (denoted by the symbol "\") must occur sequentially, and in the case of the value being taken out of the buffer, this incrementation must occur *after* the value has been taken by the consumer process.

This solution is still not entirely satisfactory, however, because whenever $n > 0$, the second alternative of the **ALT** can be selected. If this happens and the process being guarded by this condition begins to execute, it will reach the point where it is offering a value on the channel *outch* and will halt there until the consumer is ready to receive the offered value. This effectively prevents the buffer process from continuing until the value has been taken. In the worst case, the process will be deadlocked at that point, if no process wishes to take the value. Even if there is a consumer process operating, the behaviour of the buffer will be to take one value from the producer and immediately offer it to a consumer. Only in the undesirable situation where there is a continuous stream of values being provided by the producer(s) *and* the underlying scheduling policy gives preferential treatment to the first alternative of the **ALT** clause will the buffer ever contain more than one or two values!

By pursuing the analogy with the previous solutions, we can see a way of getting around this problem. Monitors (and their variants) are all passive objects, and thus it is necessary for the consumer process to ask explicitly to obtain an element from the buffer. Even in the ADA case, where the buffer is managed by the passive task, the consumer process must request that the next value in the buffer is to be delivered. In the case of the OCCAM program above, we allow the buffer, which is now an active component of the program, to offer elements rather than to be asked for them. It would not be unreasonable, however, for the OCCAM buffer to require that any consumer process wishing to remove an element from the buffer should positively request the next element rather than to expect it to be offered. Thus it would not be inappropriate for the buffer process to wait until the consumer requests an element before the "output" arm of the ALT statement could be selected. The value received from the consumer is of course irrelevant, but the buffer does need to know that

```
ALT
    (n < nmax) & inch?b[p] = >
        PAR
            n := n + 1
            SEQ
                p := p + 1
                p := p \ nmax
    (n > 0) & outch?ANY = >
        PAR
            n := n - 1
            SEQ
                outch!b[c]
                c := c + 1
                c := c \ nmax
```

Program 6.25

a request has been made, and this could be detected by the presence of an input (*any* input) on the output channel. The relevant part of the revised solution is presented as program 6.25. The purpose of the construct *outch*!ANY is to allow for the situation where the

communication *event* is of interest, whereas the *value* of the message is
not, and may be discarded

This solution is perfectly acceptable in that it performs the
required task, and it also mimics the solutions presented earlier in the
chapter. However, as we pointed out before, OCCAM is a language in
which successions of active elements are encouraged, and so it would
appear that a more natural OCCAM solution is to iterate or replicate a

```
WHILE true
VAR x:
    SEQ
        inch?x
        outch!x
```

Program 6.26

simple (one-place) buffer element. The operation of such a one-place
element is illustrated in program 6.26, and is represented
diagrammatically in figure 6.2

Figure 6.2

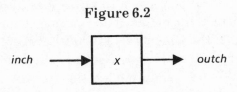

Then all that is required to turn this into an *n*-place buffer is to
chain together *n* such elements as shown in figure 6.3.

Figure 6.3

In order to represent this construction in OCCAM, we have to
introduce one other feature of the language, namely the *replication*
facility. This enables us to specify that multiple copies of a particular
construct are required. The revised program is shown as program 6.27.
Notice that the **FOR** construct does not imply a looping operation, but
rather a textual replication similar to a macro expansion.

PAR $i = [0$ **FOR** $n]$
  WHILE *true*
  VAR x:
  SEQ
    $ch[i]?x$
    $ch[i+1]!x$

Program 6.27

Notice that we have here been able to use the "control variable" of the iteration to vary the channel's use for input and output in each of the components of the expansion. The only modification of the producer and consumer processes which arises from this change is that the producer now sends items to the channel $ch[0]$ instead of *inch*, and the consumer receives them from $ch[n]$ rather than *outch*. Using this arrangement, we obtain something similar to the hardware *FIFO* component which acts as a first-in-first-out buffer, exactly as we wish the bounded buffer to behave. We also notice that our objection to the first version of the OCCAM bounded buffer has also been removed. Since each element of the buffer chain can only contain a single item, clearly we can offer the contents of that buffer element as soon as it has been delivered from the previous element. Thus the element at the front of the buffer can simply offer the item it contains to the consumer, and will only accept an item from the next element when the consumer has removed the offered item. Each item as it is offered to the buffer by the producer, will propagate along the chain until it reaches the first free buffer element, at which point it will stop pending the removal of an item by the consumer. When this happens, all the remaining items in the chain will move along one place, creating one more empty element. If this causes the element at the back of the chain to be emptied, then the producer is free to submit another item to the buffer. In a conventional (sequential) programming language, all the additional copying of elements which such a method implies would represent a considerable overhead in the operation of the buffer, but in OCCAM, this additional effort is carried out without delaying either the producer or the consumer by elements which would otherwise be idle.

6.8 Exercises

6.1 Design a Concurrent Pascal program to provide an implementation of multi-element queues.

6.2 Describe the essential differences between the condition variables in a Hoare-style monitor, and those found in the Mesa monitor construct. Explain also why the use of Hoare's condition variables has an effect on the order in which processes are executed, and why this is not the case with the use of condition variables as found in Mesa.

6.3 A Path Pascal program wishes to read information from a terminal. Before it does so, it must first *claim* the terminal, then print a *prompt*, after which it *reads* input from the terminal. When it has completed its read operation, it must *release* the terminal in order to make it available to other processes. Write down a path expression which enforces this sequence of operations.

6.4 Figure 6.9 ((a) and (b)) showed a solution in Path Pascal to the bounded buffer problem for multiple producers and consumers. The problem of interference between simultaneous *put*s or *get*s was avoided by using the path

path 10: (1: (*put*); 1: (*get*)) **end**

i.e. by allowing only one *put* and one *get* to be active at any time. By inspection of the code, however, it can be seen that interference will only occur if simultaneous accesses are attempted to the same buffer slot. Show how a Path Pascal object (and path expression) may be constructed which controls the incrementation of the *get* and *put* buffer pointers (the variables p and c in program 6.9(b)) so that multiple simultaneous calls to *put* and *get* may execute safely, and show how this object would be used in the bounded buffer object to achieve this relaxation in the concurrency constraints. What path would now need to be associated with the bounded buffer object?

6.5   Write a server task in ADA to control access to a resource which allows multiple simultaneous *read* operations, but requires exclusive access to the resource during *write* operations (i.e. write an ADA program to solve the readers and writers problem).

6.6   An ADA task is required to handle output to a printer. In order to print a file, a process must first claim the use of the printer, then print out the file and finally release the printer. This task should therefore offer to its clients three entry points, *Acquire*, *Print_File*, and *Release*. A successful *Acquire* operation should grant ownership of the printer to the calling process, and no other attempt to acquire the printer should be allowed to proceed until the current owner has performed a *Release* operation. Show how the ADA **select** statement would be used to provide this facility.

6.7   With reference to example 6.6, explain why an attempt to acquire the printer while it is owned by another process must be regarded as different from the case when a client attempts to perform the *Print_File* and *Release* operations without first completing a successful *Acquire*. How does this difference become apparent in the way the ADA program is written?

6.8   Describe how the Pascal-m model of inter-process communication (i.e. mailboxes as first class objects) could be used to provide the facilities of a client/server type interaction.

6.9   Following on from the exercise 6.8, how would you provide a name server in Pascal-m?

6.10   Write an OCCAM process which takes input (integer) operands on two channels, and then offers the sum of these on an output channel.

Write similar processes for the difference, product and (integer) quotient of two input operands.

6.11 Using separate processes to provide the values 1, 2, 3, etc., and the processes written in the answer to exercise 6.7, write an OCCAM program to evaluate the expression:
(6 + 4) * 3 - 8 / 5 + 1

6.12 The Dutch Flag Problem - Dijkstra.
$3n$ people are standing in a line. n of the people hold a red card, n of them hold a white card and the remaining n hold a blue card. By exchanging cards only with their immediate neighbours, the cards must be moved around between people so that the red cards are held by the n people at the left-hand end of the line, the white cards by the n people in the middle of the line, and the blue cards are held by the right-most n people.
By considering each person in the line as an OCCAM process, describe the algorithm which these processes would have to implement in order to ensure that the cards finish up correctly ordered.
(Notice that the people at each end of the line are special cases, and will require modifications to the general algorithm.)

6.13 An extended version of exercise 6.12 can be used to sort numbers. Instead of being coloured red, white or blue, the cards are numbered. The exchanges now have to take place to ensure that the cards are finally in numerical order (either decreasing or increasing). Again considering each card holder as being represented by an OCCAM process, describe the algorithm to be implemented by each process.

6.14 Group Communication.
A *graph* consists of a set of *nodes* and a set of *lines* joining pairs of these nodes. It is not necessarily the case that every pair of nodes has a line joining the points. A graph is said to be *connected* if it is possible to move from any node in the graph to any other node by traversing a sequence of lines (or *path*).
Such a graph might represent a group of people in which there

is a line joining node A to node B if and only if person A knows person B. (We assume that if A knows B, then B knows A.) A particular person in the group wishes to ensure that each member of the group receives a certain message. The algorithm for each person (apart from the originator) is as follows:

1. Await the arrival of the message.
2. If this is not the first time the message is received, acknowledge the message immediately.
3. Otherwise, forward the message to each person known, except the person from whom the message was originally received, and await an acknowledgment.
4. When all such acknowledgments have been received, acknowledge the arrival of the message.

The originator merely sends the message to each person he or she knows, and awaits acknowledgments from them all. When this has happened, the message has reached everyone in the group.

Write an OCCAM process to reflect this behaviour.

6.15   A *tree* is a connected graph as described in the exercise 6.14, but with the property that there are no cycles in the graph, i.e. each node is connected to every other node by exactly one path.

A *spanning tree* for a directed graph is any tree having the same set of nodes as the graph.

Devise a modification of the algorithm in the previous exercise which will find a spanning tree for a given graph.

[Hint: start with an arbitrary node, and add lines to the spanning tree until you know that each node is reachable from this node, but only by a single path.]

7
Implementation of a Concurrency Kernel

We introduce here a simple concurrency kernel, showing how it may be used to provide pseudo-concurrency on a single processor, and also in the chapter we shall show how some of the concurrency constructs introduced in chapters 4 and 5 may be implemented.

We assume that the machine on which the kernel is to be implemented consists of a single processor of the conventional type with a single monolithic address space. A simple Motorola M68000 based system would be an appropriate type of system on which to run the kernel. To make the kernel more useful, it would be possible to consider hardware which provides a virtual address translation capability, in which case the various processes could be provided with distinct address spaces in which to operate. This, however, not only makes the kernel more complicated, but also makes sharing of memory more difficult. For the purposes of the simple kernel which we are considering here, we shall assume a single (shared) address space.

The implementation language will be Pascal, and for simplicity we shall assume that a hypothetical Pascal machine has been implemented on top of the basic hardware. Apart from the ability to run Pascal programs, we shall also require some additional features to support the concurrency kernel to be constructed. It is clear that much of the underlying support, both for Pascal itself and for the concurrency kernel, will have to be provided through a small amount of assembly code. Given the Pascal machine abstraction, we can assume that the Pascal process can be represented by a state record such as was described in chapter 2.

The simplest kernel we can imagine is one in which a number of processes (say 3) are to be multiplexed on a single processor, but apart from this they are totally independent. We shall also assume that they consist of infinite loops, and that they perform no input/output operations. Clearly, on real hardware, once such a process begins to occupy the processor, it will only cease to do so if it wishes (and is provided with the necessary primitives). Alternatively, there may be some part of the underlying kernel which is able to force a return from the process to the kernel. One such mechanism would be an *interrupt*.

7.1   The "Good Citizen" Approach

Let us assume for the moment that, although the processes are completely independent of one another, they are aware of each other's presence. In the first version of the kernel, the processes have available to them a primitive operation called *Yield*. We also assume that this operation is called by each of the processes at some convenient point. The result of calling *Yield* is not apparent to the process calling it, but it gives the kernel an opportunity to hand the processor to a different process if it should wish to do so. A procedure describing how a typical process might behave is given as program 7.1.

```
procedure ProcessCode;
begin
    { initialisation code }
    repeat
        ...;
        Yield
    until false
end;
```

Program 7.1

We are now ready to make some preliminary definitions, and to describe some important primitives which our Pascal machine will need to provide. Firstly, we require the following Pascal definitions:

```
const  MaxProcess         = 3;     { for example }


type   Memoryptr          = ...;   { machine dependent }
       State              = record
                              pc, sfb, tos:  Memoryptr
                            end;
       ProcessId          = 1..MaxProcess;
       ProcessTableEntry  = record
                              procstate: State;
                              ...
                            end;
       ProcessTable       = array ProcessID of
                              ProcessTableEntry;
       WorkArea           = record
                              addr: Memoryptr;
                              size:  integer
                            end;
```

We also require the following primitive procedures (assumed to be supplied by the Pascal "hardware"):

```
function NewProcess (  procedure  ProcessCode;
         workspace: WorkArea; var initst: State):  ProcessId;
procedure Continue (st: State);
procedure GetState (var st: State);
```

The function *NewProcess* is the primitive required to create a totally new process. In calling this function, we supply a procedure *ProcessCode* to represent the code we wish the process to execute, and we supply the specification of an area of memory in which it is to execute (i.e. in which its stack is to be set up). We assume that initially the entire memory is owned by the kernel, and that the kernel is therefore free to decide how much memory to allocate to a process, and where in memory that space is to be. The side effect of *NewProcess* is to set up a new Pascal stack within the defined work area, and then to return via the variable parameter *initst* the initial state of the newly created process. It also returns, as the result of the function, a value which is the identity of the process. This value is required to be unique, in the sense that no two processes may be assigned the same value by *NewProcess*, and for convenience it is arranged that the first call to *NewProcess* will return the value 1, and from each subsequent call, the value returned will be one greater than the value returned by the previous call.

We are now ready to describe the initialisation which is required to start the kernel, and to create a set of processes. Just as we assumed that the processes are programmed as infinite loops, so the kernel is an infinite loop, passing control to each process in turn, and waiting until it receives control back, at which time it passes control to the next process in sequence, with the first process being considered to follow the last process, thus forming a cycle. With the definitions as given above, the kernel is initialised as shown in program 7.2.

In this code, we see that the kernel has allocated three regions of memory, represented by the three variables *ws1*, *ws2* and *ws3*. It has also created three processes, using three calls to *NewProcess*. In these calls, it is assumed that the procedure representing the code has the form shown in program 7.1. After each process has been created, we assume that the variable *p* contains the unique identification of that process, and that *initst* contains its initial state. It is then necessary for the corresponding process table entry to be set up with the value of that initial state, as shown.

Having created the required number of processes, and set up the process table correctly, mechanisms are now required to pass control to a process given its current state, and to retrieve the state of a running process when it is suspended (by a call to *Yield*). We assume that the underlying Pascal machine provides two primitives to do this, represented by the procedures *Continue* and *GetState* whose declarations we have already seen. Since we assume that the kernel is also to be a Pascal program, there has to be the notion of a kernel stack, which is used whenever the kernel is running. The kernel passes control to a process by suspending its own state, and establishing the state of the chosen process. Subsequently, the process returns control to the kernel by re-establishing the kernel stack, and making the state of the suspended process available to the kernel to be stored back in the process table.

program *Kernel*;

    { definitions as before }
    var   *p*:   *ProcessId*;
         proctable: *ProcessTable*;
         ws1, ws2, ws3: *WorkArea*;
         initst: *State*;

    { code for processes 1, 2, and 3 respectively }
    procedure *ProcCode1*;   ...;
    procedure *ProcCode2*;   ...;
    procedure *ProcCode3*;   ...;

begin
    { initialisation code }
    p := *NewProcess* (*ProcCode1*, *ws1*, *initst*);
    proctable [*p*].*procstate* := *initst*;
    p := *NewProcess* (*ProcCode2*, *ws2*, *initst*);
    proctable [*p*].*procstate* := *initst*;
    p := *NewProcess* (*ProcCode3*, *ws3*, *initst*);
    proctable [*p*].*procstate* := *initst*;
    p := 1; { select first process to run (arbitrarily) }

    repeat
        { kernel main loop }
    until *false*
end.

Program 7.2

Thus, the action of the procedure *Continue* is to hide the state of the kernel in some secret place known only to the kernel, and to pass control to the process whose state is passed as the parameter of *Continue*. To the kernel, this call of *Continue* is a procedure call, and the kernel would expect to regain control as though a normal return from *Continue* had occurred.

The actual return to the kernel is effected by the running process making a call to *Yield*, which in turn calls *GetState*. The result of this is to cause the kernel state to be restored in such a way that it appears that a normal procedure return from the original call of *Continue* has been made. At the same time, the state of the now suspended process is returned as the **var** parameter of *GetState*, such that when that process is eventually restarted, it appears as though a normal procedure return from *Yield* had occurred. In effect, the kernel and the process regard each other as co-routines. It would be inappropriate to give any further discussion of the implementation of *Continue* and *GetState* at this point, because the precise details are very much dependent upon the architecture of the underlying (real) processor.

Program 7.3 shows how *GetState* and *Continue* would be used,

```
procedure Yield;
var st:    State;
begin
    GetState (st);
    proctable [p].procstate := st
end;

begin
    ...
    repeat
        { kernel main loop }
        Continue (proctable [p].procstate);
        p := NextProcess (p)
    until false
end.
```

Program 7.3

but it should be noted that *Continue* is called directly by the kernel, whereas *GetState* is called (indirectly) by the process. However, *GetState* must still be regarded as a kernel procedure, and is only called by the processes as a result of their calling a kernel supplied procedure, in this case, *Yield*.

The function *NextProcess* in the kernel main loop is simply an encapsulation of the scheduling decision-making code - i.e. the code used to decide which process should be the next to run, and perhaps the simplest possible version of such a procedure would be represented by:

> **function** *NextProcess* (*p*: *ProcessId*): *ProcessId*;
> **begin**
> > *NextProcess* : = (*p* **mod** *MaxProcess*) + 1
> **end**;

i.e. the process to be selected is the next one in sequence, wrapping around when the last one is reached. Notice that while any process is running, the kernel variable *p* contains the identity of that process, and is used when the kernel regains control to identify the correct entry in the process table where the state of the suspended process must be stored. The value of *p* is then altered by the scheduling policy (procedure *NextProcess*), and this identifies the process table entry where the state of the next process to run is to be found.

7.2 Interrupt Handling

We have assumed in the previous section that all of the processes running under the control of the kernel are aware of each other's existence, and are prepared to behave like good citizens. A system in which processes are willing to behave in this way, and to give up control voluntarily is called a *non-pre-emptive* system. It is not always the case that the processes can be trusted to behave in this way, especially if the processes themselves are liable to contain errors. A much more robust system is possible if the kernel is able to *pre-empt* the running process, that is, to suspend the running process and return control to the main loop of the kernel even without the explicit co-operation of that process. Processes running within systems of this type can be truly independent of each other and need not even be aware that other processes exist.

The only way in which this can be achieved, however, is to arrange that some external event will occur and cause control to be taken from the running process and passed back to the kernel. The hardware representation of such an event is the *interrupt*. Conventionally, an interrupt in the hardware causes the processor not to execute the next (machine) instruction in sequence, but to branch to an instruction which has previously been associated with that interrupt. Enough state information is saved when this happens, that when the interrupt processing is complete, an instruction similar to a sub-routine return instruction can be executed to allow the interrupted program to continue. In other words, the code which constitutes the interrupt processing code, or *interrupt handler*, behaves like a sub-routine which is called at an unexpected moment.

We can adopt the same point of view in respect of our hypothetical Pascal machine. The interrupt-handling routine behaves like a procedure which is called when the interrupt occurs, rather than being explicitly called by the running program, and when the interrupt procedure returns, the main program continues as though nothing had happened. It is clear that this would have to be a parameterless procedure, but it would normally be declared in such a way that it could alter the values of global variables, and thus make the main program aware that it had been called. We do have to assume that the underlying Pascal machine provides a mechanism for associating a procedure with an interrupt. This might be represented by the following:

```
type Interrupt = ...;  { machine dependent - in many
                         machines it is called a vector and is
                         actually a memory address }
var int:Interrupt;
procedure IntHandler; ...;  { body describes action to be
                              taken when interrupt occurs }
procedure PlantInterruptHandler ( int: Interrupt;
                         procedure handler);
```

The procedure *handler* is provided by the user, and the procedure *PlantInterruptHandler* is part of the underlying system.

Suppose now that the machine on which our kernel is to run consists of a single processor (as before) and a timer or clock, which generates an interrupt at regular intervals, for instance, every 100 microseconds. If the processes running under the kernel either have no facilities for relinquishing control of the processor, or for accidental or malicious reasons fail to do so, then the kernel can arrange things so that it regains control as a result of an interrupt from the timer. Thus, we might have the definitions:

var *clockint*:   *Interrupt*;
procedure *ClockHandler*; ...;

and during the initialisation of the kernel, we should have to make the procedure call:

PlantInterruptHandler (*clockint, ClockHandler*);

to associate the handler procedure with the interrupt. We should also have to ensure that the timer was enabled to generate interrupts. These two statements would have to be included in the kernel initialisation (see program 7.2) immediately prior to the entry to the main loop. It transpires that if the action required by the kernel whenever a clock interrupt occurs is to suspend the current process, then the body of the procedure *ClockHandler* is identical to the body of *Yield*, since all that is required is for control to be returned to the kernel, and the state of the suspended process stored in its correct place in the process table. We assume here that it is required to switch to the next process every time the timer interrupts. If this generates too many process switches, it would of course be possible for the *ClockHandler* to update a global variable which counts the "clock ticks", and only switch processes when a certain number of ticks had occurred. So, for instance, if as before the timer generates an interrupt every 100 microseconds, but we wish to allow each process to continue for 500 microseconds before it is required to relinquish the processor, then the *ClockHandler* procedure would only call *GetState* to return control to the kernel on every fifth occasion on which it was called.

7.3   Undesirable Interference

In the preceding discussion, the assumption has been made that either the processes will co-operate in the "good citizen" fashion, or they will be subject to interrupts from a device such as a timer. In a sense, this is a reasonable assumption, since the use of a clock and interrupts would appear to make it unnecessary for processes to call the *Yield* procedure.

It may be, however, that the concurrency kernel might wish to make the *Yield* procedure available as a system facility, thus offering the processes the opportunity of voluntarily giving up control, even in a pre-emptive system. Whatever the reasons may be, it could be disastrous if processes were permitted to call *Yield*, and interrupts were able to occur as well.

If we look again at program 7.3, in which the procedure *Yield* is defined, we observe that *GetState* is called as the first executable statement. Now suppose that it so happened that the procedure *ClockHandler* were to be called after *Yield* had started executing, but before the *GetState* had been called. The body of *ClockHandler* is identical to that of *Yield*, and hence by the time *Yield* was resumed and the *GetState* within *Yield* is called, *GetState* has already been called by *ClockHandler*, and the state that is returned to *Yield* is the newly re-established kernel state. The situation which follows would be, to say the least, unpredictable, and since *Yield* would go on to save the kernel state in the process table entry belonging to the suspended process, restarting that process correctly would now be impossible.

A possible solution to this difficulty would be to introduce an additional variable into the kernel which recorded whether or not the system thought it was within the kernel or not. But the question is immediately raised as to where such a variable might be set and unset. Suppose an additional variable *kernelstate* is declared:

var *kernelstate*:   *Boolean*;

which is defined to be *true* when the kernel is executing, and *false* when a user process has control. The purpose of this variable is to avoid calling *GetState* if the kernel has control, and thus the statement:

```
begin
    if not kernelstate then
    begin
        GetState (st);
        proctable[p].procstate := st
    end
end;
```

would need to replace the body of the procedure *Yield*, and the same alteration will be required for procedure *ClockHandler*. The question still remains, however, as to where is the proper place to set and reset this new variable. Given that interrupts can occur at arbitrary times during the execution of unprotected code (i.e. most of the code we have described), it is possible to imagine a situation, wherever the variable *kernelstate* is updated, which will lead to incorrect behaviour. For example, suppose we decided that the statement:

$$kernelstate := true;$$

was required before every call of *GetState*, and suppose also that a timer interrupt occurred during the call of *Yield*, after the test of *kernelstate* had taken place, but before *GetState* was actually called. We should be no better off than if we had not made the test at all!

If we examine all the possible places where this statement might be inserted, we come to the conclusion that none of them is correct. The only possible solution is to make the setting of *kernelstate* part of the *GetState* operation, and to make the whole operation indivisible. (In fact, as a precaution against programming errors while the kernel was under development, the original version of *GetState* was arranged to be a null operation when called with *kernelstate* set to *true*. This had the added advantage that it could be a private variable to the underlying Pascal support system, set by *GetState* and reset by *Continue*, and the ability of the Pascal kernel to access the variable became unnecessary.)

7.4 The Ready Queue

While the kernel has only to concern itself with processes which are always able to run (if they are not actually running), the *NextProcess* procedure quite satisfactorily moves on from one process to the next in an orderly manner. We may wish to alter this policy, and be able to change the order in which the processes are given to the processor. One reason for wishing to do this might be that the processes should be allowed to run according to some priority rule, or, as we shall see in the next section, they may be unable to run for a time. A more flexible method of allocating the processor would be to have a *queue* of ready processes, to add processes to the tail of the queue as they leave the processor, and to select the process at the head of the queue to be the next running process. Unless some other action is taken, the process which has been in the *ready* state for the longest period of time is the next to run, as it would be in the simple version of the kernel in the previous section. We now have the flexibility, however, to alter the order of the processes in the queue should that be thought to be desirable.

In order to represent the action of a queue, following Brinch Hansen, we assume the following extension to Pascal. For any base type T, the construct:

queue of T

may be used as a constructor for a queue of elements of type T. Only two operations are allowed on variables of type **queue of**, and they are:

procedure *Add* (*item*: T;   **var** q: **queue of** T);

and:

function *Remove* (**var** q: **queue of** T): T;

The procedure *Add* simply adds *item* to the tail of the queue q, and *Remove* takes the item from the head of q and returns it as the value of the function. Both procedures have the side effect of altering the queue.

The present simple version of the kernel may now be re-written making use of the queue construct. Firstly, we require the declaration:

var *readyq*: **queue of** *ProcessId*;

Instead of selecting the next process to run by incrementing the variable p by 1, the processes will now be held in a queue of ready processes. The procedure *NextProcess* now becomes:

```
function NextProcess (p: ProcessId): ProcessId;
begin
    NextProcess := Remove (readyq)
end;
```

and the procedure *ClockHandler*, (and equivalently the procedure *Yield*) will now have as its body, the statement:

```
begin
    GetState (st);
    proctable[p].procstate := st;
    Add (p, readyq)
end;
```

7.5 Co-operation between Processes

The two mechanisms discussed so far in this chapter both assume that there will be no interaction (except inasmuch as they have - knowingly or unknowingly - to share the same processor) between any of the processes. We now need to consider the mechanisms required to implement inter-process communication and co-operation. Of course, if we assume that our hardware behaves in a reasonable manner with regard to the relationship between interrupts and memory accesses, then we could write processes using, for example, Peterson's solution, and thus solve the critical section problem. By "a reasonable manner" we mean that interrupts only take effect between machine instructions, and hence do not interfere with an individual memory access. We observe that, under this assumption, a single processor system does not even require the memory interlock, although a multiple processor system would.

In our discussion of Peterson's solution (chapter 3), we noted two significant disadvantages; firstly, it was a rather complicated solution and would therefore be liable to errors if the writer of the process code were to be expected to include it, and secondly, and more importantly, Peterson's method would require the processes to include a "busy waiting" loop. Quite apart from the efficiency disadvantage which the busy waiting mechanism introduces, we observe that if processes only relinquish the processor voluntarily, i.e. the kernel operates a non-pre-emptive scheduling policy, then a busy waiting process would never give up the processor, and no progress would be made by any process. It would be quite possible to suggest that the busy loop should contain a call to the procedure *Yield*, and thus the process would give up control each time it found itself unable to make progress, but even so, a large amount of computation would be wasted while processes were waiting for other conditions to be met.

As we discussed in chapter 3, a much better method of providing inter-process communication is to offer a *semaphore* type, with the operations *wait* and *signal* which may be performed on semaphores. The co-operating processes then must agree on the use of a particular semaphore for each interaction. To provide an implementation of the semaphore and its operations, we have to re-examine the assumptions we have made about the processes. In what we have said so far in this chapter, we have assumed that the only reason for a process to be delayed is because it is waiting for the processor to be allocated to it. That is, each process is either *running*, or it is *ready to run*. The action of a process when it performs a *wait* on a semaphore, is to indicate to the underlying system that it is unable to continue unless a particular condition is satisfied. If the condition is not satisfied, then the process is *blocked* until some other event occurs, and would be unable to run, even if the processor became available. The occurrence of the event which unblocks a process is of course the *signal* on the same semaphore by another process.

In the kernel main loop, a procedure *NextProcess* was called to determine which was to be the next process to run. In the implementation shown in section 7.1, we simply selected the next process in sequence, secure in the knowledge that it would be ready to run. In section 7.3, the *NextProcess* procedure was modified to use a queue of *ready* processes. If we introduce semaphores, we can no longer be sure that the selected process is able to continue, since it may have performed a *wait* on a semaphore, and hence blocked itself. It therefore becomes necessary to store some information somewhere which can be used to decide whether a process can run or not. We have already introduced a data structure which contains an entry for each process, and this would seem to be an obvious place in which to store this additional information. Thus, the process table entry will now be extended to contain a field to indicate whether the process is *running*, *ready* or *blocked*. Our type definition now becomes:

```
type ProcessTableEntry  =  record
                           procstate: State;
                           runstate: (running,
                                      ready,
                                      blocked);
                    end;
```

With this extension, we may still use the simple form of the procedure *NextProcess*, but modifying it to become:

```
function NextProcess (p: ProcessId): ProcessId;
begin
    repeat
        p := (p mod MaxProcess) + 1
    until proctable[p].runstate = ready;
    NextProcess := p
end;
```

Actually, with this modification only, the value of *runstate* will never be *running* for any process. In fact, this does not affect the performance of the kernel, and the running process can always be identified by the variable *p*, but for reasons of absolute completeness, we may wish to include in the main loop of the kernel a statement which assigns the value *running* to *runstate* in *p*'s process table entry prior to the call *Continue* (*p*). If the running process is suspended as a result of a timer interrupt, or by calling *Yield*, the value of *runstate* must also be changed from *running* to *ready*. This change then must be made to the bodies of both *ClockHandler* and *Yield*.

      Let us now consider what action must be taken when a call is made to *wait* on a semaphore, and also the action of *signal*ling. Not only does the version of the kernel which incorporates the semaphore construct require queues for selecting the next process to run, but when a process *signal*s on a semaphore, it may have to select which of possibly many processes waiting on the semaphore is to become ready. (Recall that each *signal* only satisfies one of the *wait*s which may have been performed on the semaphore.) The fairest algorithm for selecting which process to unblock would also be one in which the selected process would be that which has been waiting the longest. The use of a queue associated with each semaphore would suggest itself. Semaphores would thus appear as:

```
type Semaphore  = record
                     count: integer;
                     waitq: queue of ProcessId
         end;
```

For the moment we will ignore the operations required to initialise a semaphore, and concentrate on the two operations *signal* and *wait* which the active processes will wish to call. The definitions of these two procedures are given as programs 7.4 and 7.5

```
procedure wait (var s: Semaphore);
var st: State;
begin
   with s do
   begin
      count := count - 1;
      if count < 0 then
      begin
         GetState (st);
         proctable[p].procstate := st;
         Add (p, waitq);
         proctable[p].runstate := blocked
      end
   end
end;
```

Program 7.4

Several points need to be made in connection with these two procedures. Firstly, we observe that the general structure of these operations is very much like the original definitions for semaphores given in chapter 3. This is hardly surprising. Secondly, we note that in each case, if the condition is tested and is found to be false, the calling process returns immediately after updating the variable *count*. If,

```
procedure signal (var s: Semaphore);
var st: State; cand: ProcessId;
begin
    with s do
    begin
        count := count + 1;
        if count < = 0 then
        begin
            GetState (st);
            proctable[p].procstate := st;
            proctable[p].runstate := ready;
            cand := Remove (waitq);
            proctable[cand].runstate := ready
        end
    end
end;
```

Program 7.5

however, the condition is found to be true, the procedure *GetState* is called, and the process has to relinquish the processor. In the case of *wait*, this obviously must happen, since the process will become *blocked*, and be unable to continue. In the case of *signal*, however, we could have made the decision to allow the calling process to carry on, since *signal* does not block its calling process, but instead we have decided that a kernel entry will occur and that the signalling process will relinquish the processor.

In the procedure *signal*, both the signalling process and the signalled process have to be marked as *ready*, the one having come from the *running* state and the other from the *blocked* state. In fact, both of these processes should also have been added to the ready queue, so that in this case, the two statements:

proctable[p].runstate := ready;

and:

proctable[cand].runstate := ready;

must be followed by:

> $Add\,(p, readyq)$;

and;

> $Add\,(cand, readyq)$;

respectively. Another scheduling decision to be made here concerns whether the signaller or the signalled should have priority, and this will determine the order in which these two calls of Add should appear in the procedure body.

7.6   Monitors

Semaphores, as we saw in chapter 3, are quite adequate as a mechanism for providing inter-process communication, since they can be used to exchange timing information, they can provide mutual exclusion, and they can be the basis of a message passing system. However, some more structured synchronisation mechanisms were introduced in chapters 4 and 5, and it is instructive to examine how semaphores might be used to handle the implementation of such structures.

We shall begin by considering the monitor. The first constraint imposed by the monitor is that only one process shall be inside a monitor procedure at any one time. This part is easy to implement. All that is required is a semaphore to provide the mutual exclusion, called a *monitor lock*. A *wait* on the monitor lock is called at the entry to each of the monitor procedures, and a *signal* is called on exit. The signal and wait operations on a condition variable are almost as simple, except that we must be careful to observe the difference between a condition wait and a semaphore wait. We are not permitted to store signals on conditions in the same way that signals on semaphores can be accumulated. A *signal* on a condition variable for which no process is waiting is equivalent to a "no-op", and a *wait* on a condition variable will always wait, irrespective of the number of signals previously performed on that condition. Thus to implement a condition variable in terms of a semaphore, and in particular the *signal* and *wait* operations on it, we must be permitted to examine the value of the semaphore *count* field before either the *wait* or *signal* is carried out. Thus, suppose that a monitor contained the declaration:

> **var** *c*: *condition*;

then the implementation would first of all contain a semaphore, such as:

> **var** *csem*: *Semaphore*;

and the statements:

> *c.wait*; and *c.signal*;

which presumably would appear somewhere inside the monitor code, would be replaced by:

> **if** *csem.count* $< = 0$ **then** *wait* (*csem*);

and:

> **if** *csem.count* < 0 **then** *signal* (*csem*);

respectively.

Actually, the tests being performed here are identical to those being made inside the semaphore *wait* and *signal* procedures, and thus it would seem to be unnecessary to invoke the full power of *signal* and *wait*. For this reason, and for other reasons which will become clear later, it is appropriate for the queuing and de-queuing to be done explicitly in the implementation of *c.wait* and *c.signal*.

Unfortunately, this is not the whole solution, because a process executing the *c.wait* statement must be inside the monitor, and if it simply waited on the condition semaphore, it would still be holding the monitor lock, thus preventing any other process from entering the monitor. Neither is it simply a question of releasing the monitor lock just before calling *wait* (*csem*), because when another process executes the corresponding *signal* (*csem*), the process which is woken up by this action would merely join the other processes competing to enter the monitor. The assumption is made that if a process is awoken from *c.wait*, the process *knows* that the Boolean condition being tested is now true, and hence does not require to be tested again. The implication of this is that any process being awoken by *c.signal* must have priority over processes newly arrived and attempting to start execution of a monitor procedure. Not only that, but it must also have priority over the process calling *c.signal* in order to prevent this process from invalidating the Boolean condition before the newly awoken process has a chance to regain control.

The solution to this problem is to allow the signalling process to hand over control of the monitor lock to the signalled process without going through the normal *signal* and *wait* mechanism on the monitor lock semaphore. The signalling process has entered the monitor, and therefore holds the monitor lock. Without performing a *signal*(*mlock*) it could merely leave the monitor and then attempt to re-enter it by a *wait*(*mlock*). The signalled process, meanwhile, simply continues without having to perform a *wait*.

Before describing the code to implement the condition mechanism, let us briefly return to the discussion of the data structure used to describe a monitor condition variable. Because of the similarity between semaphores and conditions, it is tempting to try to use semaphores in the implementation of conditions. The difference between semaphores and conditions, however, is that it is not possible for a condition to "store up" signals for processes which will execute a *wait* later. In other words, the *count* part of the semaphore is only required to test whether or not a process is waiting. Thus, a more satisfactory way to represent a condition is to use a queue, provided we also allow a program to test to see if the queue is empty or not. Accordingly, let us extend the set of operations which may be performed on a variable of type **queue of** *T* (for some type *T*) to include the predicate (or Boolean function):

function *empty* (*q*: **queue of** *T*):   *Boolean*;

which returns the value *true* if there are no items in the queue *q*, and *false* otherwise. Now the implementation of *condition.wait* is simply a matter of the process attaching itself to the appropriate queue, marking itself as blocked, and releasing the monitor lock.

Condition.signal is implemented by the calling process inspecting the queue, making the process at the head of the queue ready (if the queue is not empty), and suspending itself on the monitor lock. This is sufficient, since it already owns the monitor lock, and therefore calling *wait* again is guaranteed to cause this process to wait. The signalled process is allowed to continue, not by having a *wait* signalled, but by inheriting the monitor lock from the signalling process.

In detail, if we assume the following definitions:

var *readyq*: **queue of** *ProcessId*;   { as before }

var *condq*: **queue of** *ProcessId*; { representing the condition }
var *mlock*: *Semaphore*:   { the monitor lock semaphore
                                which should be initialised to 1. }

the implementation might appear as calls to the procedures *ConditionSignal* (*condq*) and *ConditionWait* (*condq*), where the definitions of these procedures are given as programs 7.6 and 7.7.

```
procedure ConditionSignal (var cq: queue of ProcessId);
var cand: ProcessId;
begin
   if not empty (cq) then
   begin
      cand : = Remove (cq);
      Add (cand, readyq);
      proctable[cand].marker : = ready;
      wait (mlock)
   end
end;
```

Program 7.6

Notice that in the procedure *ConditionWait*, the signalling on the monitor lock must be programmed explicitly. This is because a normal *signal* on a semaphore will perform the necessary *GetState* operations, and mark the signalling process as *ready*. In this case, the *GetState* has already been done, and the process marked as *blocked* before the monitor lock signal is executed.

```
procedure ConditionWait (var cq: queue of ProcessId);
var st: State; cand: ProcessId;
begin
    GetState (st);
    proctable[p].procstate := st;
    Add (p, cq);
    proctable[p].marker := blocked;
    mlock.count := mlock.count + 1;
    if mlock.count < = 0 then
    begin
        cand := Remove (mlock.waitq);
        proctable[cand].marker := ready;
        Add (cand, readyq);
    end;
end;
```

Program 7.7

There is no difficulty caused by the fact that *ConditionSignal* merely places the signalled process on the ready queue, since the validity of the Boolean expression for which the signalled process was waiting can only be affected by other processes who have indicated their intention to enter the monitor. Amongst this set of processes, the signalled process is the only one which can be in a position to make progress. Any other process which may also be on the ready queue at this time will not be attempting to interfere with the data of the monitor. From this we can see that this implementation of the monitor's condition variables will work correctly.

The only remaining slight misgiving one may have is that a process signalling a condition will, as a result of performing the signal, not only lose the processor, but be relegated to the back of the monitor lock queue. This may seem a little unfair, but the method works correctly in the sense that all the concurrency constraints are met, even though the signalling process may be thought to have been discriminated against. This difficulty may be overcome, but only by introducing a priority mechanism into the scheduling, and this simply introduces more complexity into the program, which at this stage we are anxious to avoid.

7.7 Path Expressions

In chapter 4, we showed how path expressions could be used as an alternative to monitors, and how it was possible to specify more precisely the concurrency constraints, and indeed the sequentiality constraints, on the operations associated with a data structure. Path expressions provided the opportunity for concurrency and ordering constraints on the operations beyond the pure mutual exclusion offered by the monitor. We also saw how path expressions removed the need for the monitor's condition variable.

In this section we show how it is possible to use semaphores to exercise the same control over the path operations, and it follows from this that it would be possible to write a "compiler" to transform a path expression into the correct sequence of semaphore operations to be included in the prologue and epilogue of each operation.

The first observation to be made is that the simple expression:

path p **end**

where p is any path expression, implies no constraints at all, and therefore no special prologue and epilogue are required. In general, though, any arbitrary path expression p will require a prologue operation, P_p, and an epilogue operation, E_p, associated with it. The prologue will consist of some combination of *wait* operations on one or more semaphores, and the epilogue will contain corresponding *signal* operations.

We shall construct the required prologues and epilogues by considering the various ways in which paths themselves are constructed. Firstly, let us consider the sequentiality operation. Recall that a path of the form

path $a; b$ **end**

implies that the operation b may not be executed until the operation a has been completed. (Recall also that a and b could themselves be paths.) There is no other constraint implied by this path, and thus as many simultaneous activations of the pair a then b as are desired may be in progress at any given time. In order to guarantee the sequentiality of the operations a and b, we introduce a semaphore *seq*, whose initial value is zero, and arrange that the epilogue for a (E_a) contains the call *signal* (*seq*), and that the prologue for b (P_b) contains *wait* (*seq*). This ensures that no b operation may begin until a corresponding a operation has been completed, as required by the definition of the semi-colon operator in a path.

The next path construct to be considered is the "comma" construct, such as the path:

path a, b **end**

The meaning of this path is that a or b may be selected for execution, and no other constraints are implied. The implementation of such a construct is straightforward, and all that is required is for the prologue and epilogue of the path (if any) to be copied into the prologues and epilogues of the component operations (or paths).

The implementation of the restriction construct:

path N: a **end**

is achieved by introducing a "mutual exclusion" semaphore, *res*, to control the level of concurrency within the path. In the discussion of the meaning of the semaphore value in chapter 3, it was observed that the initial value of the semaphore represents the quantity of the resource which is initially available. In the case of path expressions of this type, the constant N represents the maximum number of simultaneous activations of the operation a which are permitted. If we regard N as representing the number of resources which are available for executing a, then we can see that initialising the semaphore to the value N will achieve precisely the effect we desire. After the initialisation of the semaphore, we require that the prologue of the path controlled by the restriction should contain a call to *wait* (*res*), and the epilogue should contain a corresponding *signal* (*res*).

The final path construct which was introduced in section 4.5 was the so-called "burst" mode. This was represented by the use of the square bracket notation:

path [*a*] **end**

and the meaning of this construct was that if one activation of the operation within the bracket was in progress, then another could start, but if all activations ceased, then this element of the path was regarded as having terminated. Constructing non-trivial examples of the use of burst is not easy, and on many occasions the simple choice ("comma") appears to be indistinguishable from burst mode. The real power of the construct is to make multiple activations of an operation appear to be a single activation, as in the solution in section 4.5 of the readers and writers problem. As a reminder, we recall that the path used to describe the concurrency requirements in that example was:

path 1: ([*read*], *write*) **end**

the interpretation of which was that either a single activation of *write*, or a burst of *read*s was permitted, but not both. The implementation of such a mechanism is a little tricky, because there may be, in the prologue to the path defining the burst, a *wait* on a semaphore restricting the number of simultaneous activations of the operation. In the case of the burst, however, the purpose of the construct is to allow multiple activations, even though a restriction has already been placed on the number of activations. Thus it is necessary to replace the simple *wait* (*sema*) operation with a more complex procedure that takes account of the number of currently active invocations of the enclosed operation. The epilogue will contain a corresponding *signal* operation. It is also necessary to introduce a counting variable to keep track of the number of simultaneous activations.

The simplest way to describe the necessary prologue and epilogue for burst mode is to define two procedures *StartBurst* and *EndBurst*. With each burst construct, a count is defined and initialised to zero. Since the updating of this count will occur during the prologue and epilogue of the shared operation *a*, it will also be necessary to protect the updating from undesirable simultaneous access, and hence another semaphore is required. Let us define the count to be the variable *BurstCount*, and the protecting semaphore *Mutex*. The two procedures are therefore:

```
procedure StartBurst (var sema: Semaphore);
begin
    wait (Mutex);
    BurstCount := BurstCount + 1;
    if BurstCount = 1 then wait (sema);
    signal (Mutex);
end;
```

and:

```
procedure EndBurst (var sema: Semaphore);
begin
    wait (Mutex);
    BurstCount := BurstCount - 1;
    if BurstCount = 0 then signal (sema);
    signal (Mutex);
end;
```

The parameter in each of the procedures is the semaphore which would ordinarily appear in the prologue (or epilogue) as the argument of a *wait* (or *signal*). Notice that *StartBurst* and *EndBurst* must replace these calls.

7.8   Message Passing

We have dwelt at length in previous chapters on the subject of message passing, and indeed have already shown some possible implementations of, for example, the bounded buffer in terms of semaphores. We therefore need only to make some very general remarks about implementation for these constructs.

7.8.1   OCCAM

In simple cases, such as the message passing facilities of OCCAM, it is possible to implement a channel in terms of a single memory location controlled by a single semaphore. Then, the OCCAM statements:

$$ch?v \quad \text{and} \quad ch!e$$

(assumed to be within two parallel tasks) could be replaced by:

begin *wait* (*chfullsem*); $v := chloc$; *signal* (*chemptysem*) **end**;

and:

begin *wait* (*chemptysem*); *chloc* := e; *signal* (*chfullsem*) **end**;

respectively, where the variable *chloc* represents the memory location being used as the communication channel, and *chemptysem* and *chfullsem* are the semaphores which control the use of this location by the concurrent processes. The required initialisations would be to set *chemptysem* to one, and *chfullsem* to zero. Unfortunately, this is not quite a correct implementation, because it will allow the sending process (the process executing *ch!e*) to continue without having to wait to synchronise with the receiving process. However, this is easily overcome by implementing *ch?v* by:

begin *signal* (*chemptysem*); *wait* (*chfullsem*); $v := chloc$ **end**;

and initialising both semaphores to zero. In this way, we can ensure that each process correctly waits for the other when input and output along the same channel are required.

7.8.2 ADA

In many ways, the interaction between tasks in ADA is very similar to that of OCCAM. When an active task calls an entry point in a passive task at a rendezvous, the call and the parameters may be thought of as a message. There is no buffering of such calls, and therefore a mechanism very similar to that described above for OCCAM will provide the necessary synchronisation. In the case of ADA, however, the calling (active) task is not permitted to continue until the whole of the rendezvous is complete, and therefore the signal which allows the active task to continue must be delayed until the completion of the rendezvous code.

To give a very small example, consider the tasks given in programs 7.8 and 7.9. Program 7.8 is an active task which wishes to

```
task ActiveTask;

task body ActiveTask is
    ...
    PassiveTask.EntryPt (pars);
    ...
end ActiveTask;
```

Program 7.8

```
task PassiveTask is
    entry EntryPt (pars: in out ParamType);
end PassiveTask;

task body PassiveTask is
begin
    loop
        select
            ...
        or
            when BooleanExpression = >
                accept EntryPt (pars: in out ParamType) do
                    ...
                end EntryPt;
                ...
        or
            ...
        end select;
    end loop;
end Passive Task;
```

Program 7.9

rendezvous with the passive task in program 7.9. As far as the message itself is concerned, we shall assume that the identity of the entry point being requested, and the values/addresses of the parameters involved in the interaction are all passed across to the passive task in a way similar to the mechanism by which conventional programming languages call and pass parameters to procedures. It is therefore only the synchronisation aspects of the rendezvous that need to be considered here. The active task calls for a rendezvous in exactly the same way as a program in a sequential programming language calls a procedure. It will be necessary, however, for the entry point call to be preceded and followed by appropriate synchronisation operations. These will be similar to those described above for OCCAM, viz.

$$...; SetUpCall; signal\ (rvreq); wait\ (rvcomplete); ...$$

which simply informs the passive task of its desire to execute a rendezvous, and then waits until it is complete. Because the active task has nothing to do while the rendezvous is in progress, we have been able to use the same semaphore to indicate that the rendezvous is taking place and to indicate the completion of the rendezvous.

The situation for the passive task is very similar. The **accept** statement cannot be executed until a rendezvous is requested by an active task, and therefore, its first action must be to *wait* on the semaphore *rvreq*. Once this *wait* has been satisfied (i.e. by a *signal* in some active task), the **accept** statement will first have to discover which of the several possible entry points is being selected, then whether or not the associated Boolean guard (if there is one) is true, and if possible to execute the rendezvous code. Only following the successful execution of an **accept** is the passive task permitted to *signal* on the *rvcomplete* semaphore.

7.9   Exercises

7.1   Describe the changes which would be required in order to provide for each process to be selected for execution according to a fixed priority.

7.2   In the exercise 4.5 (chapter 4), which required the construction of a monitor to handle the buffering of characters being printed on a line printer, the routine *GetChar* would be called by the printer device driving process. In practice, it would probably be implemented in the form of an interrupt handler, and it would also run at higher priority than other processes, in particular the process(es) which call(s) *PutString*. Show how the routine *GetChar* can be written in the form of an interrupt handler without invoking the full facilities of the monitor construct. Show also how *Putstring* would have to be written

(a)   taking into account the fact that it could be interrupted at any time by a call to *GetChar*, and

(b)   given that it must be prepared to (re)start the device driver if it has just placed a character into an otherwise empty buffer.

7.3   Consider the problem of implementing a concurrency kernel on a number (> 1) of c.p.u.'s.

7.4   Describe how you would modify the code of *ConditionSignal* and *ConditionWait* to provide MESA-style synchronisation as distinct from the Hoare-style monitor implementation given in programs 7.6 and 7.7.

Bibliography

This bibliography does not aim to be in any way exhaustive, but just to provide a few pointers into the vast wealth of literature on the topic of concurrent programming. We begin by referring to other textbooks on the subject. As has been pointed out already (in the Preface) the subject of concurrent programming essentially grew out of a study of operating systems, and many, if not most, textbooks on operating systems include a section on concurrency. A few such text books are suggested:

Brinch Hansen, P.,
Operating System Principles. Prentice Hall. (1973).

Deitel, H.M.,
Operating Systems. Second Edition. Addison Wesley. (1990).

Habermann, A.N.,
Introduction to Operating System Design. Science Research Associates. (1976).

Silberschatz, A., Peterson, J.L., and Galvin, P.B.,
Operating System Concepts. Third Edition. Addison Wesley. (1991).

Tsichritzis, D.C., and Bernstein, A.J.,
Operating Systems. Academic Press. (1974).

By contrast, the following book begins as a textbook on concurrent programming, and develops the operating system topic towards the end of the book. It also might be regarded as the definitive reference on the language Concurrent Euclid:

Holt, R.C.,
Concurrent Euclid, The UNIX System, and Tunis. Addison Wesley. (1983).

In addition, text books devoted entirely to the study of concurrent (parallel) programming have appeared:

Andrews, G.R.,
   Concurrent Programming: Principles and Practice. Benjamin/Cummings. (1991).

Ben-Ari, M.,
   Principles of Concurrent Programming. Prentice Hall Intl. (1982).

Perrott, R.H.,
   Parallel Programming. Addison Wesley. (1987).

The following review article appeared in *ACM Computing Surveys*, and as is the nature of review articles, itself contains an extensive list of references:

Andrews, G.R., and Schneider, F.B.,
   Concepts and notations for concurrent programming. *ACM Computing Surveys* 15(1), pp. 3-43. (1983).

From an historical point of view, some of the most important contributions to the literature are the following:

Brinch Hansen, P.,
   The Architecture of Concurrent Programs. Prentice Hall. (1977).
   A comparison of two synchronising concepts. *Acta Informatica* 1, pp.190-199. (1972).

Conway, M.E.,
   A Multiprocessor System Design. *Proceedings of the AFIPS Fall Joint Computer Conference*, pp.139-146. (1963).

Courtois, P.J., Heymans, F., and Parnas, D.L.,
   Concurrent control with "readers" and "writers". *Comm ACM* 14, pp.667-668. (1971).

Dennis, J.B., and Van Horn, E.C.,
   Programming semantics for multi-programmed computations. *Comm ACM* 9, pp.143-155. (1966).

Dijkstra, E.W.,
   Solution of a problem in concurrent programming control. *Comm ACM* **8**, p. 569. (1965).
   Co-operating sequential processes. In *Programming Languages*, F. Genyus (ed.), Academic Press, pp.43-112. (1967).
   Hierarchical ordering of sequential processes. *Acta Informatica* **1**, pp. 115-138. (1971).
   Guarded commands, non-determinacy, and the formal derivation of programs. *Comm ACM* **18**, pp. 453-457. (1975).

Hoare, C.A.R.,
   Towards a theory of parallel programming. In *Operating Systems Techniques*, C.A.R.Hoare and R.H.Perrott (eds.), pp.61-71. Academic Press. (1972).
   Monitors, an operating system structuring concept. *Comm ACM* **17** pp. 549-557. (1974).

Horning, J.J., and Randell, B.,
   Process structuring. *ACM Computing Surveys* **5**, pp. 5-30. (1973).

Lamport, L.,
   A new solution of Dijkstra's concurrent programming problem. *Comm ACM* **17**, pp. 453-455. (1974).

Peterson, G.L.,
   Myths about the mutual exclusion problem. *Information Processing Letters* **12**, pp. 115-116. (1981).

The following books and articles are related to the specific languages to which reference has been made in the text. In some cases, notably ADA and OCCAM, we refer to early papers which give the initial flavour of the language. In many cases, programming texts have also been published which may be of interest to readers who wish actually to write programs in these languages.

Abramsky, S., and Bornat, R.,
   PASCAL-M: a language for distributed systems. *QMC CS Lab Report 245*, Queen Mary College, London. (1980).

Barnes, J.G.P.,
An overview of ADA. *Software - Practice and Experience* 10, pp. 851-887. (1980).

Brinch Hansen, P.,
The programming language Concurrent Pascal. *IEEE Trans on Software Engineering. SE-1* 2, pp.199-206. (1975).

Campbell, R.H., Greenberg, I.B., and Miller, T.J.,
Path Pascal User Manual. *Technical Report UIUCDCS-R-79-960*, Department of Computer Science, University of Illinois at Urbana-Champaign. (1979).

Campbell, R.H., and Habermann, A.N.,
The specification of process synchronisation by path expressions. *Lecture Notes in Computer Science* 16, Springer-Verlag, pp.89-102. (1974).

Hoare, C.A.R.,
Communicating sequential processes. *Comm ACM* 21, pp. 666-677. (1978).
Communicating Sequential Processes. Prentice Hall Intl. (1985).

Inmos Ltd,
OCCAM Programming Manual. Prentice Hall Intl. (1984).

Lampson, B.W., and Redell, D.D.,
Experience with processes and monitors in Mesa. *Comm ACM* 23, pp. 105-117. (1980).

May, D.,
OCCAM , *ACM SigPlan Notices* 18, No. 4, pp. 69-79. (1983).

Mitchell, J.G., Maybury, W., and Sweet, R.E.,
Mesa Language Manual, version 5.0. *Palo Alto Research Center Report CSL-79-3*, Xerox Corp. (1979).

Welsh, J., and Bustard, D.W.,
Pascal Plus - another language for modular multiprogramming. *Software - Practice and Experience* 9, pp. 947-957. (1979).

Welsh, J., and Lister, A.,

A comparative study of task communication in ADA. *Software - Practice and Experience* 11, pp. 257-290. (1981).

and has already been mentioned, R.C.Holt's book is the definitive textbook on the language Concurrent Euclid.

Index

RF